The Centre for Research in Ethnic Relations is a Designated Research Centre of the Economic and Social Research Council. The Centre publishes a series of Research, Policy, Statistical and Occasional Papers, as well as Bibliographies and Research Monographs. The views expressed in our publications are the responsibility of the authors.

Price: £4.00   (including handling charge and VAT)

Orders for Centre publications should be addressed to the Administrative Assistant, Centre for Research in Ethnic Relations, Arts Building, University of Warwick, Coventry CV4 7AL. Cheques and Postal Orders should be made payable to the University of Warwick. Please enclose remittance with order.

ISSN   0268 3970

ISBN   0 948303 45 X

A TALE OF FAILURE : RACE AND POLICING

CENTRE FOR RESEARCH IN ETHNIC RELATIONS,
UNIVERSITY OF WARWICK

WORKING PAPERS ON ETHNIC RELATIONS

RESEARCH PAPERS

POLICY PAPERS

1   Barry Troyna and Wendy Ball   Views from the Chalk Face:
    School Responses to an LEA´s policy on Multicultural
    Education
2   Selina Goulbourne   Minority Entry to the Legal
    Profession: A Discussion Paper
3   John Benyon   A Tale of Failure: Race and Policing

BIBLIOGRAPHIES

1   Zig Layton-Henry   Race and Politics in Britain
    (Revised Edition)
2   Anne-Marie Phizacklea   The Employment of
    Migrant/Immigrant Labour in Britain (Revised by
    John Solomos)
3   Nora Kornalijnslijper and Robin Ward   Housing and Ethnic
    Relations in Britain (Revised Edition)
4   Mark Johnson   Race and Health
5   Mark Johnson   Race and Place
6   Daniele Joly and Jorgen Nielsen   Muslims in Britain: An
    Annotated Bibliography 1960-1984
7   Mark Johnson   Race and Care

MONOGRAPHS

1   Heather Booth   Guestworkers or Immigrants?   A
    Demographic Analysis of the Status of Migrants in West
    Germany
2   Robin Ward   Race and Residence in Britain,   Approaches
    to Differential Treatment in Housing

STATISTICAL PAPERS

1   Heath Booth   Second Generation Migrants in Western
    Europe: Demographic Data Sources and Needs

OCCASIONAL PAPERS

1   John Cowley   West Indian Gramophone Records in Britain
    1927-1950
2   Centre for Research in Ethnic Relations   Research
    Programme (1985-1989)
3   John Rex   The Concept of a multi-cultural Society: A
    Lecture

REPRINT PAPERS

1   Barry Troyna   "Policy Entrepreneurs" and the Development
    of Multi-Ethnic Education Policies: a Reconstruction

NOTES ON THE AUTHOR

John Benyon is Lecturer in Politics and Public
Administration in the Department of Adult Education at the
University of Leicester. He was previously at the
University of Warwick and was a member of Warwick District
Council, 1979-1983. He edited Scarman and After
(Pergamon, 1984), and his publications include articles in
Public Administration, New Scientist, Local Government
Studies and Parliamentary Affairs. He is co-editor of The
Police: Powers, Procedures and Proprieties (Pergamon,
1986) and his research interests include politics and
order, crime and policing, inner city deprivation and
racial disadvantage.

ACKNOWLEDGMENTS

I am most grateful to Liz Kemp and Beryl Penny who typed
the manuscript. I also gratefully acknowledge the
Leverhulme Trust's award of a Research Fellowship, which
helped to finance the research and production of this
paper. It is a pleasure also to express my appreciation to
those in the Centre for Research in Ethnic Relations who
have helped me, especially John Solomos and
Professor Robin Cohen. In addition, I am pleased to thank
Zig Layton-Henry, Senior Lecturer in Politics at the
University of Warwick, for his help and support, and for
his comments on the manuscript. I would also like to
thank Dr Paul Rich for commenting on the paper, and I wish
to express my appreciation to colleagues at the University
of Leicester, especially Professor William Forster,
Professor Peter Jackson and Colin Bourn, for their support
and encouragement. Finally, I would like to thank Coleen,
Joseph and Danielle for bearing with me over a
considerable period.

A shorter version of this paper appears as Chapter 9,
'Spiral of decline : race and policing' in
Zig Layton-Henry and Paul Rich (eds), Race, Government and
Politics in Britain. London : Macmillan, 1986.

CONTENTS

1. RACE, POLICING AND THE 1985 DISORDERS

Introduction

Police officers are important and valued public servants, and indeed British society would be unimaginable without them. Their job is a difficult one, for few people like being told what to do by those in authority while most people expect to receive prompt and effective service if they need assistance by the police. Inner city areas, in particular, have never been easy to police and the pressure under which officers work in such districts is very considerable. Perhaps it is here more than anywhere that the integrity and impartiality of the police need to be assured in order to win and sustain the confidence, trust and co-operation of ordinary citizens. Above all the police must be seen as fair and just, and if this is achieved their legitimacy and effectiveness are likely to be increased.

However, a study[1] of the literature, research findings and other evidence suggests that many citizens, particularly Asians and Afro-Caribbeans, who live in the large cities of Britain do not perceive the police to be just or fair. Rather than trusting them, a significant number of people seem to mistrust and resent the police. As the Archbishop of Canterbury's Commission on Urban Priority Areas reported in November 1985:

> We have heard numerous complaints from black people of alleged discrimination against them by the police... This loss of confidence in the police, and suspicion of racial or class discrimination in methods of policing and among magistrates, can result in substantial groups in the community ceasing to regard the Law as `friend'.[2]

The evidence reviewed in this paper shows that the position is indeed disturbing. The picture which emerges is a depressing one of widespread hostility towards, and resentment of, the police. It is difficult not to conclude, as Lord Scarman did in the case of Brixton, that the history of relations between the police and black people has been largely `a tale of failure'.[3]

The paper first outlines in brief the 1985 disorders, and the reactions to them. The impact of the operation of powers of stop and search, and the variation in the rates of arrest of different ethnic groups, are then considered. This is followed by a discussion of crime, policing and young black people, looking particularly at the moral panic over mugging. A central factor seems to be the way in which race and policing went `out of court' in 1975-76, so that from this point the Metropolitan Police in particular began to highlight black crime as `a growing problem'. This change in approach by Scotland Yard, and its impact on race and policing, are examined and the paper then turns to consider allegations of police misconduct, and the evidence of the deterioration in relations between police and black people, both of which have a long history. More recently a number of police operations, such as the raids on the Mangrove Restaurant, Notting Hill, and on houses in Railton Road, Brixton, have provoked considerable outcry, but the police complaints system, before its reform in 1985, has seemingly been ineffective in commanding widespread confidence. Another area which is examined is policing and racial attacks, and here too the story is a depressing one. Evidence on the attitudes of Asians and Afro-Caribbeans reveals that they believe they are treated worse than whites by the police, and in the case of West Indian people the findings are overwhelming.

2

From the literature and research findings which are reviewed, three broad problems which adversely affect race and policing can be identified: racially discriminatory behaviour; police officers' attitudes and conduct in general; and `institutional racism'. Each of these is briefly examined, although of course policing and race cannot be isolated from the wider context within which it takes place. The paper concludes that in some areas a vicious circle or spiral of decline exists in relations between the police and significant numbers of residents, especially black people. If appropriate initiatives were firmly implemented the spiral of decline could be arrested, but the predominant responses to the 1985 riots do not augur well. Research suggests that increased force leads to more disturbances and less consent by those affected, thus exacerbating the spiral of decline. In answer to the question `is the tale of failure in race and policing set to continue?´, it is difficult to respond with optimism.

Race, policing and the 1985 disorders

Relations between the police and black people were at the centre of the serious disorders which occurred in several English cities during September and early October, 1985. As Appendix A shows, each riot was precipitated by an incident involving police officers and black people, and each occurred in areas in which there was widespread antagonism between some members of the ethnic minorities and the police.

The first eruption took place on Monday 9 September 1985 in the Lozells Road area of Handsworth, Birmingham. The riots resulted in the deaths of two Asian men, Amirali Moledina and his brother Kassamali, who suffered asphyxiation in their burning post office. Thirty other people, mainly police, were reported injured and the value

3

of damaged property was put at £10 million. Further rioting occurred the next day, when Mr Douglas Hurd, the newly-appointed Home Secretary, visited the scene. Other disturbances, widely regarded as `copycat´, were reported elsewhere in the West Midlands, for example in Moseley, Wolverhampton and Coventry, and in the St Pauls district of Bristol, which was the scene of serious disorder in April 1980.

The Handsworth/Soho/Lozells area, with a population of 56,300, is regarded by Birmingham City Council as `the most deprived district in the city´. Unemployment is a major affliction, and at the time of the riots 36 per cent of the workforce in Handsworth was out of work, while the figure for people under 24 years was 50 per cent. It is an area which has been noted in recent years for reasonably good relations between young blacks and the police, based on the concept of community policing introduced by Superintendent David Webb in the late 1970s. However, at the end of 1981 he left the police service and although his approach was continued by his successor he, too, moved from the area in April 1985. The new superintendent instituted changes which included moving a number of the area´s community police officers to other duties, and clamping down on activities by local youths which had previously been tolerated. In particular police attention turned to the use of cannabis by black youths, and a number of raids took place during the summer. For example, on 10 July 150 officers raided the Acapulco cafe in Villa Road, and seven people were arrested.

These changes in officers and tactics resulted in an increase in tension between youths and the police. In July 1985 two serious disturbances occurred in Handsworth, but both were played down and went unreported by the media. In the first, about seventy youths rioted, attacking police vehicles and officers and looting a shop. It took over two hours to restore order. A few days

4

later, police officers who were questioning a youth were
attacked by a large group of young people. The context
within which the eruption occurred on 9 September was thus
one of deteriorating relations between young people,
especially blacks, and the police, as well as one of
widespread unemployment and social disadvantage. The
tinder merely required a spark, which was provided when a
black youth became involved in an altercation with an
officer over a parking ticket. It is alleged that during
the incident, at which more police arrived, a black woman
was assaulted, but whether or not this occurred what is
certain is that two hours later some 45 buildings in
Lozells Road were ablaze.

Brixton was the scene of the next outbreak of
violent disorder, during the weekend 28-29 September 1985.
Police reported 724 major crimes, 43 members of the public
and ten police officers were injured, and 230 arrests were
made. As in Handsworth, the trigger event which led to
the rioting involved police officers and a black person,
on this occasion Mrs Cherry Groce. At 7am on 28
September, armed police entered her house in Normandy
Road, Brixton, looking for her son. Two shots were fired
by an officer, and a bullet damaged Mrs Groce's spine
causing permanent paralysis. At 6pm the local police
station was attacked with petrol bombs, and during the
next eight hours large numbers of black and white people
took part in burning and looting which caused damage
estimated at £3 million. During the riot a freelance
photographer, Mr David Hodge, sustained injuries from
which he died three weeks later.

Two days after Mrs Groce was shot, rioting occurred
in Liverpool 8. In this instance, the disturbances were
precipitated when four black men were refused bail at
Liverpool Magistrates' Court. They had been charged in
connection with a fracas in August, but local youths
claimed that they were being treated unfairly and picked

5

upon by the police. During the summer there were reports of rising tension in the area, and on 30 August a crowd demonstrated outside Toxteth police station, and then attacked police cars and the station itself. A number of assaults on police officers were also reported. As in Brixton and Handsworth, police relations with young people, and especially black youths, was a significant factor in the explosive mixture, and in Toxteth, too, the disorder was precipitated by an incident involving police officers and black people. Quite why rioting occurred in Peckham in London, on the same night, is not clear. The context seems to be similar to the other instances, that is one of rising tension between young people and the police, and at about 10pm on 30 September the centre of Peckham was effectively sealed off for at least four hours. Police reported `various sporadic acts of lawlessness´, and it was reported that many people, especially blacks, were prevented from returning to their own homes.

The most serious of the disorders occurred at Broadwater Farm Estate, in Tottenham, London. The rioting began at about 6.45pm on Sunday 6 October 1985, and during a night of extraordinary violence PC Keith Blakelock was stabbed to death, 20 members of the public and 200 police officers were injured and a large number of cars and some buildings were burned. Guns were fired at the police, causing injuries to several officers and reporters, and the police deployed CS gas and plastic bullets, although these were not used. A first-hand account of the events was given by Steve Platt in New Society :

> `The flames scorched the front of our house´, Pantelis Georgiou told me when I took refuge there at the height of the trouble ... `All we could see was a sheet of flame. The next thing I knew the street was full of 250 or 300 people, throwing whatever they could find at the police...´

> Evdokia, his wife - shaking and scared, as the battle raged outside - peered into her back garden while we talked. Rioters had torn down

6

and burnt the fence. There was no longer
anything between us and the Broadwater Farm
Estate's Willan Road, where the worst of the
fighting was underway and - unbeknown to us - a
policeman was being knifed to death ...

A black couple trying to leave the area via
Willan Road were turned back at the police
lines, to a chorus of the monkey noises used to
abuse black footballers by racists at soccer
matches. `Fuck off niggers', yelled one of the
policemen. `Go back and live in the zoo. You
can burn that down'. `Go back in your rat hole,
vermin', echoed another. `We'll be in to get
you soon enough' ...

Whatever the underlying causes of the riot,
there was no denying the intoxicating thrill it
offered as relief from everyday life on the
dole. All over the estate, crowds of bystanders
and onlookers were gathered. `It's better than
the telly, isn't it?', said one old lady, who
appeared to be taking her dog for a walk in the
midst of this curious mixture of madness, mayhem
and the oddly mundane ...4

The next day, the Metropolitan Police Commissioner,
Sir Kenneth Newman, stated:

Yesterday evening the ferocity of the attack on
the Metropolitan Police was senseless and beyond
belief ... To write off such acts as directly
attributable to a lack of jobs, or facilities or
past unfairness is to indict all those who are
unable to work or who are black, white or poor,
but do not sink to such depths.

Petrol bombing, arson and looting are alien to
our streets. They must not go on. Last night I
deployed members of my Tactical Firearms Unit in
readiness to use plastic bullets. They were not
used, because the containment operation, though
grave in its economic and human costs, was
successful.

But, I wish to put all people of London on
notice that I will not shrink from such a
decision should I believe it a practical option
for restoring peace and preventing crime and
injury. I would have hoped not to have had to
express that thought, but yesterday evening's
events have made it a regretable possibility.

The Home Secretary said that he fully supported Newman, and so with the ferocious events at Tottenham the use of plastic bullets on the streets of Britain have become a real possibility.

As in Handsworth, Brixton and Toxteth, the context within which the disturbances occurred in Tottenham was one of deteriorating relations between the police and young people, especially blacks, and the trigger event involved police officers and black people. The chief superintendent for the area, Colin Couch, is a strong believer in community policing, and he put as his first priority the prevention of public disorder. However, it is clear that many of his police constables and sergeants did not agree with his approach.

During the summer of 1985 there was evidence of increasing tension, and a prominent member of the Hornsey Police Federation was quoted as saying that the rank and file officers `desperately wanted to go in hard and sort out the criminals´. Some serious incidents occurred during this period on the Broadwater Farm Estate, such as an attack on police by youths which resulted in one officer sustaining a bad head wound, and there was also a series of attacks on an Asian-owned supermarket. Senior police officers appeared to play these incidents down, but black youths complained that off the estate they were increasingly harassed by the police. During the week before the riots a stop and search operation was conducted at the entrance to the estate, and young blacks said that they were unfairly picked on and subjected to abuse and rough treatment. On 9 January 1986, a report prepared by Michael Richards, a Deputy Assistant Commissioner at Scotland Yard, was presented to the Haringey Police-Community Consultative Group. The report confirmed that tension between the police and youths in the area was increasing for some time before the riot was triggered. It concluded that the disorder was planned, rather than a spontaneous reaction, but the account given was clearly partial in that the views of non-police eyewitnesses were excluded. On 13 January 1986 Mr Bernie Grant, leader of Haringey Council, again called for an independent public inquiry into the disorder but this was promptly dismissed once more by the Home Office Minister, Giles Shaw. It does seem incredible that rioting as serious as that which occurred has not been investigated by an official inquiry, and one can only wonder at the Government's stance on this.

The incident which triggered the riots began when police officers stopped a car driven by Floyd Jarrett, a 23 year old black man, who is well-known in the area as a worker at the Broadwater Farm Youth Association. In the BMW car with Jarrett was his pregnant girl friend. The police officers stopped him because his tax disc was out of date, and he explained that this was because he had only just returned from a youth exchange trip to Jamaica. The officers searched his car for stolen goods, but Jarrett says that he became concerned about his girl friend and requested to move off. A row developed which ended with Jarrett being arrested for assaulting a police officer, although he and his girl friend denied that any such assault took place. In court, he was later acquitted of the charge. What happened after Jarrett arrived at the police station is subject to dispute. The arrested man claims that he was assaulted, detained for five hours without being allowed to make a phone call, and then released with his possessions returned to him minus the front door key to his mother's house. The police stated that he was treated correctly. The Jarrett family claim that five police officers used Floyd's key to enter his mother's home, whereas the police stated that they found the door open. Some weeks later, at the inquest into the death of Mrs Jarrett, police officers admitted that this story was untrue.

9

During the police search of the house, Mrs Jarrett collapsed and died. The family alleged assault by police officers, and negligence in summoning an ambulance; the police firmly denied this. The incident occurred during the early evening of Saturday 5 October 1985, and the story spread round the estate during the evening. The next day, after sporadic anti-police incidents, violent disorder erupted.

Reactions to the 1985 riots

The riots in 1985, like those in 1981 and 1980[5], provoked a variety of explanations. Much of the press seemed particularly attracted by the conspiracy theory and the Daily Express, in its `Tottenham Riot Special,´ edition of 8 October, managed to reach new depths of fantasy. Under its headline Moscow-trained hit squad gave orders as mob hacked PC Blakelock to death KILL! KILL! KILL!, the Express explained:

> The thugs who murdered policeman Keith Blakelock in the Tottenham riots acted on orders of crazed Left-wing extremists.
>
> Street-fighting experts trained in Moscow and Libya were behind Britain´s worst violence.
>
> The chilling plot emerged last night as detectives hunted a hand-picked death squad believed to have been sent into North London hell-bent on bloodshed.

Many police officers, while not going as far as the press, suggested that agitators had fostered the disorder. Mr Norman Tebbit ascribed the riots to `wickedness´, but, as a correspondent to The Guardian remarked, if riots are caused by wickedness the stock of human wickedness must have risen alarmingly since the election of Mr Tebbit´s Conservative Party to government. Douglas Hurd, Home Secretary, said after the Handsworth disorder that it was `not a social phenomenon but crimes´.

Some Labour Party politicians such as Roy Hattersley and Jeff Rooker seemed to agree with Mr Hurd in the aftermath of Handsworth. More generally though, the response from Labour Party speakers, and from those in community groups, local government, the churches, trade unions and from some police officers, was to stress social deprivation, racial disadvantage and unemployment as causes of the disorders. Gerald Kaufman asked how, if the disorder was simply crime and not related to other social and economic factors, it occurred in areas such as Handsworth, Brixton and Tottenham but not in the delightful area of Witney in Oxfordshire, which is the Home Secretary's constituency. Mr Neil Kinnock attacked the Government's complacency, and the cuts in support for councils running the inner city areas; it was, he said, government by `lethargy and conflict'.

Kaufman's remarks seem well made for, as in 1981, the areas which experienced disorder in 1985 share common characteristics. Unemployment is high, particularly amongst the young and especially amongst young black people. Housing is poor and often overcrowded, environmental decay is evident, social problems are widespread and facilities are poor. A high proportion of the population in each area is Afro-Caribbean or Asian, and these are the people who tend to experience the social and economic disadvantages particularly acutely, and who are subjected to racial discrimination, racist abuse and on occasions physical attacks. These areas are also characterised by relatively high levels of crime, and by the use by some young people of cannabis. There is however little evidence of a major hard drugs problem in the areas in which disorder occurred in 1985, despite media assertions to the contrary.

Handsworth, Brixton, Liverpool 8 and Tottenham also seem to share two other characteristics. First, they are areas where political disadvantage is widespread in that

there are few institutions, opportunities and resources
for articulating grievances, and for bringing pressure to
bear on those with political power. Many citizens in
these areas lack the resources to voice politically their
demands and complaints, and hence they are politically as
well as materially dispossessed. The second common
characteristic of these areas is that allegations of
police misconduct have been frequently made in the recent
past, tension between police and youths - especially
blacks - has been rising and there is evidence of police
`heavy-handedness´, if not downright harassment.
Lord Scarman found all these factors evidence in Brixton
in 1981, and he stated:

> Taken together, they provide a set of social
> conditions which create a predisposition towards
> violent protest. Where deprivation and
> frustration exist on the scale to be found among
> the young black people of Brixton, the
> probability of disorder must, therefore, be
> strong.6

His remarks can be applied with equal force to the areas
in which disorder occurred in 1985.

2. STOPS, SEARCHES AND ARRESTS OF BLACK PEOPLE

It was commonly argued that police behaviour was the principal factor which had created the potential for disorder and also triggered actual rioting. Police harassment and misbehaviour, it was claimed, provided the tinder and then the spark to ignite it. Lord Scarman reported in 1981:

> The riots were essentially an outburst of anger and resentment by young black people against the police.7

'Indignant and resentful against the police'

In 1985, too, many considered the disorders should be interpreted in this way, but the context of social deprivation and disadvantage, and especially the very high levels of unemployment, seems to have been a key factor.8 It is undeniable, though, that policing was perceived as a major grievance, especially by young black people living in the areas where the riots occurred. In 1981, in Brixton, Lord Scarman seems to have been genuinely shocked at what he found:

> Many of the young, particularly (but not exclusively) the young of the ethnic minority, had become indignant and resentful against the police, suspicious of everything they did.9

Similar views had been expressed about the St Paul's district of Bristol in which major disorder occurred on 2 April 1980.10 Here, as in Brixton almost exactly a year later, a confrontation between police officers and local young people led to the riots. In 1981, in Liverpool 8 it was claimed that 'everyone on the streets had a personal grudge against the police'11 and in Moss Side, Manchester, where serious disorder began on 8 July 1981, the district police station was the prime target of attack. A

reporter, Michael Nally, who was present during this riot
was in no doubt that the youths were on the streets `to
protest against alleged harassment and ill-treatment by
the police´. One youth put forward the views of many:

> I´m here to see the pigs get theirs. They´ve
> done this for years. Now they know what it´s
> like to be hit back.12

The participants in the 1981 disorders, like those
in 1985, were both black and white, despite media
assertions to the contrary. Almost 4,000 people were
arrested during the disorders in July 1981 and, of the
3,704 for whom data are available, 766 were described as
`West Indian/African´, 180 as `Asian´ and 292 as `other or
not recorded´; some 2,466, or 67 per cent, were described
as `white´. These figures varied from area to area; while
in Toxteth and Moss Side the proportion of those arrested
who were `non-white´ was about a third, in Southall and
Brixton it was around two-thirds. Nearly seven out of ten
of those arrested were under twenty-one years of age.[13]

The poor relations between police and young black
people in certain areas has been highlighted in a number
of studies.[14] In particular friction has occurred between
police officers and young blacks on the streets, where
powers to stop and search people and to arrest individuals
`on suspicion´ have been employed. Section 4 of the
Vagrancy Act 1824 enabled police officers in London, and
in some other large cities such as Manchester and
Liverpool, to arrest and charge someone with being a
suspected person loitering with intent to commit an
arrestable offence. The burden of proof on the police was
very low and not only was it not necessary to produce the
potential victim of the alleged crime or a witness but,
indeed, this was rarely done. It was claimed, and widely
believed, that police officers abused the legislation and
used it to keep young black people off the streets.
According to George Greaves, Principal Community Relations
Officer in Lambeth:

So apprehensive had some parents become that
their children might be charged as suspected
persons that they either kept them indoors,
particularly after dark, or arranged for them to
be escorted by an adult if they had to be out.[15]

In some areas, then, it appears that by the late 1970s it
was regarded as unsafe to let teenagers go out to their
youth clubs, church events and similar activities for fear
of police harassment, and so the confidence of members of
the community in policing was eroded yet further.

A detailed study of the `sus´ law found that of the
2112 people arrested in London in 1976 under this
legislation, 42 per cent were black - a strikingly high
figure.[16] A Home Office Research Study revealed that a
black person was <u>fifteen times</u> more likely to be arrested
for `sus´ than a white person.[17] The growing discontent
with this position led the Home Affairs Select Committee
in 1980 unanimously to recommend repeal of the
legislation[18] and this was put into effect by the Criminal
Attempts Act 1981.

The `substantial cost´ of stops and searches

General stop and search powers have in the past been
provided for certain police forces such as those in
London, Merseyside and the West Midlands, and all
constables in England and Wales have now been given the
power to stop and search a person or a vehicle for stolen
or prohibited articles as long as they have `reasonable
grounds for suspicion´. These extended powers are
provided in sections 1-3 of the Police and Criminal
Evidence Act 1984, which came into effect on 1 January
1986.

There is considerable evidence that stop and search
powers are disproportionately applied to young people, men

15

and Afro-Caribbeans. In Liverpool it was reported that the powers were being increasingly used, and were causing friction between young people and the police, and data from Birmingham and Manchester showed high stop rates among young and Afro-Caribbean people.[19] Carole Willis' study in 1982 of four police stations also found that the stop rates for black people were far higher than for the population as a whole, and in Kensington the stop rate for black males aged between 16 and 24 was three times that for all males in this age group. Willis also reported that the recorded statistics under-estimate the number of stops by about fifty per cent.[20]

The most detailed data come from the Policy Studies Institute (PSI) study of the Metropolitan Police.[21] They show clearly that the chances of being stopped by the police are strongly related to age, sex, ethnic group and use of a vehicle. Young black people are likely to be stopped repeatedly, and have a far higher chance of being stopped on foot than young whites: 45 per cent of West Indians aged 15-24 had been stopped during the previous year compared to 18 per cent of white people in the same age group. The data showed that Afro-Caribbean people were `markedly less happy' than white or Asian people with the behaviour of the police who stopped them, and this was particularly `evident amongst young blacks. The findings suggest that about one and a half million stops are made by the Metropolitan Police every year, and these result in about 75,000 people being reported for offences, which are usually traffic violations, and a further 45,000 individuals being arrested and charged. Overall the study found that 8 per cent of stops produce a `result', and this proportion is the same for each ethnic group. The researchers report that

> the cost of the present policy, in terms of the relationship between the police and certain sections of the public, is shown to be substantial, and most stops are wasted effort, if they are seen as purely an attempt to detect crime. The findings therefore sugggest that the police should look for other more efficient and less damaging methods of

16

crime detection to replace those stops that are currently carried out for no very specific reason: It may be significant, in this connection, that in some other parts of the country the clear-up rate is higher than in London although many fewer stops are carried out.22

The validity of these remarks was demonstrated by the infamous operation, known within the police as Swamp '81, which was taking place at the time of the Brixton riots. The purpose of this operation was to detect and arrest burglars and robbers on the streets of Lambeth. One hundred and twelve officers were involved and the strategy was to flood particular areas with police who would make extensive use of the stop and search powers. During the course of Operation Swamp, from 6 April to 11 April 1981, 943 stops were made. Over two-thirds of those people who were stopped were aged under 21, and over half of those stopped were black. One hundred and eighteen people were arrested and 75 charges resulted, but these included only 1 for robbery, 1 for attempted burglary and 20 for theft or attempted theft.23

As critics have pointed out, judged by its own aims - `to arrest burglars and robbers´ - the operation was not a resounding success and it resulted in over 850 innocent people being inconvenienced. Lord Scarman reported that `Swamp '81 was a factor which contributed to the great increase in tension´ in Brixton and, in short, it was `a serious mistake´.24

Variations in rates of arrest of ethnic groups

Black people, especially those who are male and young, are also arrested in disproportionate numbers, according to the available evidence. Stevens and Willis reported that the arrest rate for Afro-Caribbean people, in Metropolitan Police divisions in 1975, was higher than that for whites and Asians for every category of offence. The arrest rates for assault were found to be 466 per

17

100,000 population for Afro-Caribbean, 124 for Asians and 77 for whites; for robbery they were 160 per 100,000 for Afro-Caribbeans, 13 for Asians and 18 for whites; and for 'other violent theft' they were 60 for Afro-Caribbeans, 4 for Asians and 4 for whites.[25]

The Home Office researchers investigated a number of possible explanations for the undue variation. They found that to a small extent it could be accounted for by age differences: young people in general are more likely to be arrested and higher proportions of the ethnic minority communities are young. A more significant explanation was found by examining socio-economic characteristics of different ethnic groups: a high proportion of black people are found in socio-economic categories where the chances of arrest are high.

Stevens and Willis suggested a number of explanations for the variation in arrest rates which is not accounted for by socio-economic and demographic variables. Intrinsic factors may include forms of social deprivation and disadvantage which were not examined, and different tendencies to take part in crime. Extrinsic features entail the differential enforcement of the law or, put another way, a higher likelihood that black people will be picked up (rightly or wrongly) by the police. This may be because they are more likely to frequent places where arrests occur, or because the police concentrate on certain areas, types of offence and on particular sorts of people. Indeed it was found that blacks were the group most likely to be arrested for 'sus' and for 'other violent theft' (mostly snatches of wallets and handbags causing no injury) where, the researchers stated, 'there is considerable scope for selective perception'.[26] The study suggests that police bias is quite plausibly a factor in the disproportionately high arrest rates among black people.[27]

The PSI study of the Metropolitan Police also found that Afro-Caribbean people were far more likely to be arrested than those from other ethnic groups. In the survey of Londoners, 15 per cent of black men reported they had been arrested during the last five years, as compared with 10 per cent of white males. Whereas 11 per cent of 15-24 year old whites had been arrested, the corresponding figure for Afro-Caribbeans was 17 per cent.[28] The figures from the survey of police officers matched closely, with officers describing the last person arrested as Afro-Caribbean (Identcode 3) in 17 per cent of cases, although they constitute only about 6 per cent of the London population.[29]

The authors of the PSI study suggest reasons similar to those put forward by Stevens and Willis, and indeed to those advanced by the Metropolitan Police itself in evidence to the 1976-77 inquiry by the Select Committee on Race Relations.[30] Scotland Yard's statistics revealed that in 1975, 12 per cent of those arrested for indictable crime were Afro-Caribbean. The Metropolitan Police considered that this proved a disproportionate involvement in crime, and to reinforce their case they produced statistics based on victims' descriptions of their assailants. The police figures showed that 28 per cent of those arrested for robbery were `West Indian/African´, and 32 per cent of identified attackers were described as `coloured´; similarly, of the total arrests for violent thefts, 37 per cent were `West Indian/African´ and 41 per cent of identified thieves were `coloured´. Scotland Yard also invoked socio-economic and demographic explanations:

> It is no part of our position that there is a causal link between ethnic origin and crime. What our records do suggest is that London's black citizens, among whom those of West Indian origin predominate, are disproportionately involved in many forms of crime. But in view of their heavy concentration in areas of urban stress, which are themselves high crime areas, and in view of the disproportionate numbers of young people in the West Indian population, this pattern is not surprising.31

19

The Metropolitan Police were thus quite content to accept deprivationist and demographic explanations, as long as the Select Committee was made aware of 'the problem of black crime'. However, the Community Relations Commission subjected Scotland Yard's data, and their interpretation, to considerable criticism, and in this they were powerfully supported by Professor Terence Morris of the University of London.[32] He noted eight points of particular interest. First, the arrest rate of 12 per cent for Afro-Caribbeans was entirely consistent with social class variables, so race as a factor could be spurious. Second, he criticised the equation of arrests with crimes, suggesting that in many respects the number of arrests of black people is likely to be a poor index of the proportion of crimes committed by them. Third, there was no data produced by Scotland Yard to refute the view that the high arrest rate of Afro-Caribbeans was at least partly a result of discrimination by the police. Fourth, he suggested that serious and trivial offences might have been grouped together, and the figures may have been affected by the deployment of police manpower in respect of petty incidents and minor infringements - in short, police discretion was a significant factor. Fifth, he expressed surprise at the exclusion of data comparing black and non-black arrest rates for certain offences and sixth he pointed out that police methods can affect the arrest rates for some groups in particular areas:

> In the absence of data to the contrary, one must continue to examine the possibility that the arrest rates of black persons are in some part - though not of course wholly - determined by the concentration of police presence in areas in which large numbers of black persons live and/or resort.33

A seventh criticism raised by Morris concerned the reports of victims describing their assailants: it would be unwise to rely on these data as the circumstances of the particular offences of robbery and violent theft mean that identification is difficult and there are problems of selective perceptions. <u>Eighth</u>, Morris argued that the presentation and manipulation of the data was `to say the least perplexing´ and in some respects `seriously defective´.

3. RACE, POLICING AND CRIME

The arguments put forward by Morris and the
Community Relations Commission persuaded the Select
Committee 'that there is no evidence available to justify
any firm conclusions about the relative involvement of
West Indians in crime'.[34] This was rather less definite
than the Committee's conclusion in 1972 that 'the West
Indian crime rate is much the same as that of the
indigenous population'.[35] The 1971-72 Select Committee
inquiry received the views of many senior police officers,
which were that crime rates among 'immigrant groups' were
no higher, and in some cases were lower, than among white
people. Chief constables and commanders in Lancashire,
Sheffield, Leeds, Coventry, Manchester and Islington
suggested that the total crime rate amongst 'immigrants'
was lower than expected; while in Notting Hill, Wandsworth
and Birmingham the rate was about that which would be
expected according to the proportion of 'immigrants'
living in the respective areas.[36]

Policing, crime and young black people

However, by the time it presented its evidence to
the later Select Committee inquiry, on 25 March 1976, the
Metropolitan Police took a rather different stance, as
cited earlier. This has prompted authors such as John Lea
and Jock Young to ask what happened between 1971 and 1976
to alter the police position.[37] If, as claimed by many,
the disproportionately high level of arrests of young
blacks shown in the 1975 figures was a result of police

22

discrimination, it seems rather implausible, argue Lea and Young, to suggest that this was not also occurring in 1971:

> Either the police were almost entirely free of prejudice prior to 1971 and rapidly became prejudiced during the 1970s, which is rather unlikely, or their prejudice led them, in some strange way, to engage in a form of positive discrimination prior to 1971, consciously under-representing black crime and Asian crime in particular.38

Lea and Young strongly criticise the proponents of a futile `either-or´ argument which, they say, is characterised on one side by the claim that the higher arrest rate for young blacks is a result of police prejudice, and on the other by the view that it is a reflection of the greater number of crimes committed by them. They emphasise the need to see the interconnection between these two views and to appreciate three related factors.39 First, the crime rate for black people is disproportionately high and, as a result of deprivation, unemployment and discrimination,

> there was a real rise in crime among the West Indian population, and the police, in responding to it, were not responding simply to figments of their imagination.40

An important point, according to Lea and Young, is the development of cultural conditions which sanction certain kinds of crime, and hence the difference between the levels of crime committed by young Afro-Caribbeans and young Asians.

The second related factor is that at least partly because of racial prejudice the police respond readily to the rise in black crime levels. For the ordinary police officer the deprivationist arguments put forward by senior staff are of no consequence; race is seen as a cause of crime. Third, the two processes reinforce one another leading to `deviancy amplification´.41 Thus rising black crime rates and the increasing police action against young blacks become part of a vicious circle.

To some extent it would seem that Lea and Young are over-simplifying the targets of their attack, as the `either-or´ argument appears to be something of an artificial construct. To take the `either´ side first, while it is true that a few writers, such as Bridges and Gilroy,[42] have appeared to argue that the higher black crime figures are simply the result of police prejudice this would seem to be a rather unusual view. Most analysts accept that in some areas quite a number of certain types of crime involve Afro-Caribbean young people. As Stuart Hall and his fellow authors stated in 1978 about areas in some British cities:

> Black youth are clearly involved in some petty and street crime in these areas, and the proportion involved may well be higher than it was a decade earlier. Black community and social workers in these areas believe this to be the case, an impression more reliable than the figures.43

In these classic `crime-prone´ areas, unemployment is high, housing is poor, much of the population is young, and there are few opportunities for overcoming the widespread social and economic deprivation. Changes in consciousness, ideology and culture have led to less acquiescence amongst some young black people living in the `urban colonies´, and many of them have chosen separateness rather than incorporation. `Colony life´ has offered the possibility of alternative means of survival, such as `hustling´ and concurrently there has been an increased `hassling´ of young blacks by the police.[44]

Inter-generational conflict has resulted in some young people leaving home, but with few if any employment opportunities:

> This fraction of the black labouring class is engaged in the traditional activity of the wageless and the workless: doing nothing, filling out time, trying to survive.... A fraction of the class is being criminalised.

All the evidence suggests that the numbers now
forced to survive in these ways on the margin of
the legal life are increasing, directly in line
with the numbers unemployed, and that the age
limit of those involved is dropping.45

There is a danger than explanations of this kind
will be interpreted by those who so choose as excusing
crime and violence. Hall and his co-authors make it plain
that, though understandable and unsurprising, the resort
to crime by young people is divisive and if violence is
used this is disabling and degrading. Race Today
expressed a similar view:

> We are uncompromisingly against mugging. We see
> the mugging activity as a manifestation of
> powerlessness, a consequence of being without a
> wage.46

'Aliens' and crime: a 'moral panic'

The notion of 'mugging' reintroduces the 'or' side
of the debate highlighted by Lea and Young. During the
early seventies, and intermittently since, the news media,
spurred on by certain politicians, judges and police
officers, devoted considerable attention to crimes which
have popularly been termed 'mugging'. In law no such
offence exists and different people and groups use it to
include various crimes. In 1976, for example, in answer
to the question 'how many incidents of mugging have been
reported...?', a Home Office minister referred to the
4,452 cases of robbery in London during 1975.47 However,
robbery includes a number of crimes which would not
normally be regarded as 'mugging' - such as robbery from
banks and business premises.

Street robbery is not, of course, a new crime and,
as the Metropolitan Police Commissioner stated in 1964,
'London has always been the scene of robberies from
further back than the days of highwaymen and footpads'.48
One hundred years earlier, in the winter of 1862-63,

`garotting´ was a new name given to an old crime and it `created something like a reign of terror´. The Times commented that it was `un-British´, `of foreign importation´ and no doubt the result of aliens. The garotters´ behaviour, said The Times, resembled that of the `Indian "thuggee"´.[49]

The idea that an alien intrusion is causing crime and disorder has commonly been invoked by the media and politicians. As mentioned earlier, `aliens´ and `agitators´ are invariably blamed if `un-British´ behaviour such as rioting occurs, and yet evidence for such `intruders´ is seldom if ever produced. In its issue of 17 August 1972, the Daily Mirror introduced the country to a `new´ crime which was alien and un-British: `As crimes of violence escalate a word common in the United States enters the British headlines: MUGGING. To our police it´s a frightening new strain of crime.´ During the next twelve months a `moral panic´[50] occurred over `mugging´, with frequent media reports, speeches by politicians, police officers and other opinion leaders, and several prominent court cases.

Many of the incidents which were reported involved neither robbery nor violence, but theft such as pickpocketing. Although white youths were involved in a number of the cases, the predominant impression given in the media was that the perpetrators were black. This occurred in three ways: first, when the locations of street crime were reported, invariably stress was laid on the inner city areas where black people lived; second, discussions of the American experience related `mugging´ to blacks and ghettos; finally, the association was made explicit either by victims´ descriptions of their assailants or by the identifcation of people arrested and prosecuted. The `alien´ form of this `un-British´ behaviour was thus two-fold: it was an American import perpetrated by `coloured immigrants´.

26

The `mugging´ panic reappeared in early 1975 based on crime figures released by Scotland Yard. In a piece entitled `Danger signals from the streets of Lambeth´, Derek Humphry wrote in The Sunday Times that `soaring street crime´ was a result of the `widespread alienation of West Indian youngsters from white society´.[51] The Metropolitan Police figures were based on victims´ descriptions of their assailants; 79 per cent of the robberies, and 83 per cent of offences of theft from the person, were alleged to have been committed by black people. However, it was later discovered that the total number of offences upon which the robberies statistic was based was only 111, while that for theft from the person offences was 324.[52] The study was based on Brixton but the media largely ignored this context with stories such as those in The Times `mugging..[is].. increasing in South London..[and].. 80 per cent of the attackers are black´, the Evening News `80 per cent of London´s muggers are black´ and the Sunday Express `in a large part of the city 80 per cent of the muggers are black´.[53]

The release of the `black crime´ figures led to an increased focus on race, crime and policing. In May 1975, sentencing five black youths, a judge commented:

> Within memory these areas were peaceful, safe and agreeable to live in. But the immigrant resettlement which has occurred over the past 25 years has radically transformed that environment. Those concerned with the maintenance of law and order are confronted with immense difficulties.[54]

The next year, at the Notting Hill Carnival, a major confrontation took place between young people, primarily black, and the police. The district police station was besieged, 95 police officers were injured and other serious disturbances occurred. The police argued that crimes were being committed at the Carnival and according to Sir Robert Mark, the Metropolitan Commissioner, `crime is not negotiable as far as we are concerned. If there is a crime we will decide how to deal with it´.[55] The

Carnival Committee on the other hand suggested that police numbers were provocative, while black youths complained of harassment. According to the Community Relations Council events at the 1976 Notting Hill Carnival showed that relationships betwen young West Indians and the police

> have broken down to such a degree that mutual distrust, suspicion and antagonism lead to the formation of battle lines so that sometimes trivial incidents quickly escalate into open hostilities.56

Five years later Lord Scarman was using very similar terms in his report on Brixton.

Race, crime and policing 'go out of Court'

On 13 October 1976, Peckham police released a press statement prepared by Scotland Yard which detailed street crimes in the area and made reference to a large rise in 'muggings' carried out by black people, usually on white victims. The Home Office had by now attempted to offer a definiton of 'mugging' as 'an offence of robbery of personal property which follows a sudden attack in the open where there is no previous association between the victim and the assailant'57, and on this basis Sir Robert Mark estimated that in 1975, of the 4,452 cases of robbery in London, 1,977 fell into the 'mugging' category. The Peckham figures, however, seemed to include robberies and theft from the person; they were duly reported sensationally in the press as 'mugging' even though the total arrest figure upon which some of the statistics were based was just 55.

It is clear that the Metropolitan Police statistics provide a dubious basis for relating race and crime. The fact that young black people are arrested disproportionately for a number of different types of offence seems likely to be the result of several factors, of which police prejudice and stereotyping may not be the least significant. Lea and Young accept that this may be a cause but they ask, if the figures are simply a result of police activity and prejudice, how can the changes in police attitude between the Select Committee inquiries of 1971-72 and 1976-77 be explained?[58] When one examines the evidence presented to the earlier inquiry three points emerge which may help to answer the question. First, in 1971 statistics on the race of people arrested were generally not kept by police forces and, indeed, 1975 was the first year for which `identcoded´ arrest figures were made available. Thus, few meaningful comparisons can be made with the crime data reported to the Select Committee inquiry in 1976-77. Second, in those areas where evidence was available in 1971-72, arrest and charge figures often did tend to show that Afro-Caribbean people were disproportionately apprehended for certain offences. At Notting Hill Police Station, over 15 per cent of the people charged with crime were `coloured persons´. In Wandsworth 62 per cent of the 135 cases of theft from the person were `attributable to coloured youths´ in 1971, and in Moss Side it was `estimated´ that 75 per cent of crimes of violence, robbery and thefts from the person were committed by `coloured persons against white persons´.[59]

A third point which emerges from the report of the Select Committee in 1971-72 is that the views of a number of police officers differed from the orthodox opinions of the senior staff. The Committee itself reported:

> There seems to be a fairly widespread feeling, shared, as we found in informal discussion, by some police officers, that immigrants commit more crime than the indigenous population.[60]

The suggestion made by the police, and apparently supported by Lea and Young, that there was a sudden increase between 1971 and 1975 in the arrest rates of black people for some types of crime[61] appears to be founded on dubious evidence.

Indeed, in 1963 McClintock reported that the proportion of people who were convicted of violent crimes in London who were black immigrants had risen from 6.2 per cent in 1950 to 13.0 per cent in 1960.[62] By contrast, a study in Birmingham of crime rates in 1966 showed that Afro-Caribbean people were prosecuted for indictable crime at a lower rate than would be expected from their proportion of the total population. This revealed, according to the author, that black people `generally rise above the delinquent and criminal standards prevalent in the areas where they live'.[63] However, many police officers, at least at the level of constable and sergeant, seem to have believed that black people were more involved in crime than non-blacks, even though their chief officers were publicly saying the opposite. Maureen Cain, for example, found that many policemen considered that `niggers' were `in the main...pimps and layabouts, living off what we pay in taxes'[64] and some years earlier, in 1966, Joseph Hunte produced a report for the West Indian Standing Conference which alleged racial abuse, harassment and brutality by the police and a general suspicion amongst police officers that black people were criminals. The title of Hunte's report was **Nigger-Hunting in England?**, as, it was said, police officers leaving their stations were heard saying they were going `nigger-hunting'.[65]

Why, then, were senior police officers painting a much gloomier picture of race, crime and policing in 1976-77 than in 1972? Part of this change in attitude may be attributed, as Lea and Young suggest, to a growth in the number of certain types of crimes committed by young black people.[66] By 1975-76 there were more young black people between thirteen and seventeen years of age - the age group which, according to the Metropolitan Police, was the most prone to commit street crimes.[67] If the same proportion of young black people had offended in 1975 as in 1971 there would have been an increase in the number of street crimes as the total number of young blacks had increased. Furthermore, as unemployment rates had increased during this period, particularly in inner urban areas where many young black people lived, it seems plausible to suppose that this may have been related to an increase in the number of young black people who committed offences.[68]

Besides an actual change in the number of offences committed by Afro-Caribbean people, there seem to be four other possible explanations for the change in senior police officers' views between 1972 and 1976-77. First, police stereotyping and prejudice may have increased during the period, leading to a greater number of arrests of Afro-Caribbeans in 1975 than in 1971. Second, senior police officers may have become persuaded of the extent of black crime by junior officers so that by 1976-77 they were reflecting the views held earlier by constables and sergeants. Third, senior officers, concerned at the amount of criticism about harassment of black people, may have sought to defend their actions, especially their use of stop and search powers and 'sus' charges, by arguing that the involvement of Afro-Caribbeans in crime justified them. Fourth, there may have been a general change in public or elite opinion, which was being reflected in the attitudes of senior police officers in 1976-77 when they appeared before the Select Committee.

Perhaps each of these factors played a part in the decision of Scotland Yard to highlight black crime as a 'growing problem'. In Bulpitt's terms this marked a move away from the liberal language of analysis which characterised the London-oriented Political Establishment. This change in public stance by the police coincides with the period from 1976 onwards when, argues Bulpitt, important aspects of race relations tended to 'go out of Court'.[69] Before this, using an analysis based on the notion of a Centre-Periphery or Court-Country power configuration, the Centre's statecraft had reasonably successfully managed race and politics in Britain. The liberal language of analysis which emanated from the London-based Establishment (the Centre or Court) was predominant amongst politicians, bureaucrats, certain of the quality media and leaders of key institutions such as the police. This liberal approach, generally optimistic about race relations and keen to play down difficulties, was much in evidence in the proceedings of the 1971-72 Select Committee inquiry. The final words of its report illustrate this language of analysis:

> If the best examples of leadership in police and immigrant relations prevailed throughout forces in the United Kingdom, many of the difficulties we have dwelt upon would, within a reasonable space of time, diminish. In some places they could wither away.70

The Committee stressed the need for education and patience and the whole tone of their report, and of their investigations, reflected the Establishment's political approach, which was generally a call for tolerance and understanding, a hope that race relations would improve and an aspiration to keep race off the main political agenda.

However, by 1976-77 race was firmly on the agenda under the general headings of crime, law and order and policing, largely placed there by the media and the `moral panic` over `mugging`, and by the police themselves. The Centre was confronted with a position in which

> important aspects of the issue tended to go out of Court: increasingly race politics occurred outside the limited confines of Westminster and Whitehall. In other words, the Periphery's traditionally passive role of responding to Centre initiatives declined.71

`A crude equation between crime and black people´

The gloves were off and the police, especially in London, moved into action in those areas where crime was seen as a major problem - primarily areas with large black populations. Black youths in particular were regarded with suspicion and consequently stop and `sus´ legislation, were used against them more than against other groups, as the evidence cited shows.[72] Brixton was one such area where the police were determined to tackle crime. It seems that by this they meant primarily street crime, which, according to their own evidence to the Select Committee in 1976-77, they viewed as largely black crime.

Between January 1978 and September 1980 special operations against crime on the streets of Lambeth were organised on four occasions, using the Special Patrol Group. According to evidence presented to Lord Scarman by the Metropolitan Police, serious offences in Lambeth and in Brixton increased between 1976 and 1980 by 13 per cent, which was 2 per cent lower than the increase for the Metropolitan Police District as a whole. And yet the increase between 1976 and 1980 for the offences of robbery and other violent theft was claimed to be 138 per cent in Brixton compared with 38 per cent for the London area.[73] How could it be that serious offences in general rose at a lower rate than elsewhere, but robbery and other violent theft, which includes those crimes called `mugging´, rose at a much higher rate than across the whole Metropolitan Police District?

One possible answer is that a vicious circle, similar to that which Lea and Young identified, was at work: some rise in these crimes led to increasing public concern, which focussed police attention on particular areas, offences and stereotypes, namely `young black criminals.´ As Mannheim pointed out:

> Police statistics reflect the activities of the
> police at any given time and place and are,
> therefore, greatly dependent on the interest
> taken by the police in a certain type of crime
> or certain classes of persons.74

This sort of police attention and activity could have led to some deviancy amplification, as the increased police presence could have resulted in more crimes being reported. Another possibility is that police in Brixton were categorising offences differently than police elsewhere; for example crimes which in another area would have been classified as `theft´ might in Brixton have been termed `violent theft´. A careful analysis of the figures convinced Blom-Cooper and Drabble that this was indeed happening. They found that while the rate for robbery and violent theft was **higher**, the rate for `other theft and handling stolen goods´ was **lower**, than in the Metropolitan Police District as a whole.75

As a result of their statistics, the reliability of which can be seen to be suspect, the police in Brixton saturated the area on a number of occasions, and conducted frequent stops and searches, a strategy which culminated in Operation Swamp ´81. The Policy Studies Institute study of the Metropolitan Police, which was being carried out during this period, reported that

> Police officers tend to make a crude equation
> between crime and black people, to assume that
> suspects are black and to justify stopping
> people in these terms.76

Afro-Caribbean people, especially teenagers, were far more likely to be stopped than others and the effects of these special operations is `beyond doubt´, according to Lord Scarman:

> They provoked the hostility of young black people,
> who felt they were being hunted irrespective of
> their innocence or guilt. And their hostility
> infected older members of the community, who,
> hearing the stories of many innocent young people
> who had been stopped and searched, began themselves
> to lose confidence in, and respect for, the police.
> However well-intentioned, these operations
> precipitated a crisis of confidence...77

4. RELATIONS DETERIORATE FURTHER

`The Yard fights back´

Lord Scarman´s report was published on 25 November
1981, and in it he counselled caution about future `hard´
policing in view of the damage it had caused, and the
absence of any tangible benefits. However just two months
later, in what might have been considered by some as
wilful not to say arrogant behaviour, Deputy Assistant
Commissioner Gilbert Kelland was reported as telling his
divisional commanders that there should be no let-up.[78]
The report in the Daily Mail in which this appeared was
headed `More and more muggings but the Yard fights back´,
and this did indeed mark the beginning of a sustained
`fight back´ against Lord Scarman´s criticisms, and his
recommendations. On 5 March 1982 the Daily Mail carried a
double page story entitled `PRISONERS BEHIND NET CURTAINS´
and four days later the Daily Express had a similar piece
headed `ON BRITAIN´S MOST BRUTAL STREETS´. Each story was
about Brixton and each featured attacks by black youths on
elderly white women.

The London crime statistics, released on 10 March
1982, were taken up with apparent gusto by the media, and
were grossly distorted by many newspapers. In the
statistics released by Scotland Yard the race of suspects
was indicated only in cases of robbery and other violent
thefts, and the London total of 18,763 such offences
included robberies from banks and other businesses, and
non-violent thefts from the person. Indeed, it is
reported that in 90 per cent of offences classified as
`other violent theft´ no injuries whatsoever are sustained

by the victim.[79]   Furthermore,   this whole category of
crime,   subject   to so much attention, makes up just 3 per
cent of all serious crime known to the police and it might
be   reasonably   asked   why   the   other 97 per cent was not
rigorously examined by the media.   To make these points is
not   to   seek   to   condone,   or lessen the seriousness of,
street   crime,   but merely to try to place it in some sort
of perspective. This the press did not do.

The   Daily Star,   on   11 March 1982,   for example
referred   to   `the   total of nearly 19,000 muggings´, when
the   number   of   reported street robberies was 5,889. The
Daily Mail´s front   page   story   was   `BLACK CRIME: THE
ALARMING FIGURES´   and it reported that 55.42 per cent of
the   assailants   were   identified   as `coloured´ while the
`overwhelming   majority´  of the victims `are white and are
women.   All   too often elderly women´. Other newspapers
carried   similar   reports.[80]   In   short,   unscrupulous
newspapers   peddled   distorted images of crime and race in
London,   based   on   figures   released   by the Metropolitan
Police.   As one commentator in March 1982 observed:

> Londoners   riding home on the proverbial Clapham
> omnibus   - especially the Clapham omnibus - last
> week could have been forgiven for believing that
> they   resided in a city racked by racial hatred,
> where   black   muggers   loitered threateningly at
> every street corner waiting to accost them.81

In   1983   similar figures were again released `through the
malevolent   offices   of   Mr.   Harvey   Proctor,   the
ultra-right-wing Conservative MP´, reported The Guardian
leader,   which   referred   to   `selective manipulation´ and
`orchestrated distortion´ of the figures.[82]  The `popular´
press   responded again with headlines such as `BLACK CRIME
SHOCK´ (The Sun, 23 March 1983), and once more stereotypes
and prejudices were reinforced, and the fears and anger of
black people   strengthened.   Since   then,   these   crime
figures   broken   down   by   race   of suspects have not been
released   in this way, but the damage to relations between
the   police and many   black people had   already been done.

36

Allegations of police misconduct

The parlous state of relations between the police and `significant sections` of the Lambeth public was clearly apparent to Lord Scarman. He found a `crisis of confidence` and `a serious break-down in relations`; in short

> the history of relations between the police and the people of Brixton during recent years has been a tale of failure.83

Aspects of this deterioration were charted in strident terms in the report by the Working Party into Community/Police Relations in Lambeth, which was established by the Borough Council in March 1979. The position was described as `extremely grave` and the police were accused of intimidating and harassing working class people in general and black people in particular. Furthermore, reported the Working Party, they had received evidence of `violence, intimidation and induced confessions`, of extensive misconduct, rudeness and incivility.84 As Francis Wheen reported in the New Statesman

> most of the witnesses quoted in the report do not sound as though they are `anti-police` by inclination; they are simply people who have been cowed into a mood of brooding resentment.85

The working party was established in response to a request from the Council for Community Relations in Lambeth, which had resolved early in 1979 to withdraw from a formal liaison committee with the police. This liaison forum had been established only a few months earlier but had got off to a bad start when a special police operation, involving the SPG and extensive use of stop and search powers, took place three days after the inaugural meeting, at which no announcement of the operation was made. Matters deteriorated further as a result of the `Sheepskin Saga` in February 1979, when three members of the staff of the Council for Community Relations in Lambeth were arrested because they, like the alleged

37

assailants of two plain clothes police officers and a black barman, wore sheepskin coats. The report of the Working Party was published in 1981, three months before the Brixton disorders confirmed its direst warnings. Lord Scarman commented

> I have no doubt that the style, language and contents of this report succeeded only in worsening community relations with the police. But I am also satisfied that it reflected attitudes, beliefs and feelings widely prevalent in Lambeth since 1979.86

There is, however, little doubt that hostility towards the police was widespread in certain areas well before 1979, caused by incidents such as those described by George Greaves in his contribution to Scarman and After. In 1976, for example, a black man in his late fifties was walking home along Railton Road in Brixton:

> he was stopped by police and questioned about a parcel of groceries which he was carrying. He was man-handled, and his groceries scattered in the roadway. A pregnant young woman intervened but she was rebuffed with such force that she fell to the ground...87

Many specific cases of police misconduct have been documented and one of the worst is that which involved Mr. and Mrs. White of Stoke Newington in London. During the night of 15 September 1976 some seventeen police officers illegally entered the home of the elderly black couple looking for stolen goods, of which none were found. David and Lucille White were arrested and charged with assaulting police officers, for which they were subsequently acquitted. It was pointed out that Mr. White was an elderly, frail person and it was over two months before he was sufficiently recovered from his injuries to return to his work. In April 1982, hearing a claim for damages, Mr. Justice Mars-Jones adjudged that the police officers were guilty of `monstrous, wicked and shameful conduct´ and a `brutal, savage and sustained variety of assaults´, and they had `assaulted this defenceless man in his own home with a weapon and beat him up in a brutal, inhuman way.....[88] Mr. and Mrs. White were awarded damages against Sir David McNee, Commissioner of Police for the Metropolis, of £51,392.

The Whites' case was particularly horrifying but it is only one of a catalogue of cases of alleged police misconduct against black people. Some of these were cited in the evidence presented to the Royal Commission on Criminal Procedure by the Institute of Race Relations, published as Police Against Black People, and others have been documented by authors such as Derek Humphry and Paul Gordon.[89] A few cases are well known, such as that which involved the death of the Nigerian David Oluwale and led to the imprisonment of two police officers for assault. At their trial, in 1971 at Leeds, witnesses reported that the officers had repeatedly assaulted the man and one of them had urinated on him.

Relations `almost akin to civil war'

The majority of alleged incidents of police misbehaviour are, of course, more mundane and seldom reach the headlines. Many examples are contained in the evidence received by the Select Committee inquiries in 1971-72 and 1976-77, and, to take just one example, the memorandum submitted by the West Indian Standing Conference on 27 January 1972 was described by William Deedes MP, Chairman of the Select Committee, as presenting `a case almost akin to civil war between the West Indians and the police'.[90] In 1976 a member of the Committee, Dudley Smith MP, felt it it necessary to inform the President of the Association of Chief Police Officers of the views of the Afro-Caribbean representatives:

> There has been a consistent, continuous allegation on the part of many of the witnesses appearing before us that they are discriminated against by the police. The more reasonable

witnesses say that officers, very senior
officers like yourself and other reasonably
senior officers, understand the problem and
honestly and genuinely to the best of their
ability try to operate non-discrimination and
the equality of the races. They say that on the
other hand, down the line the young policeman
and the not so young policeman on the beat or on
patrol does not; that he discriminates against
blacks; that he does not like blacks; that he
regards them as inferior citizens and says in
fact, `What the hell are you doing here? We do
not want you`....the main discrimination alleged
in this country is largely that allegedly
committed by the police.91

Many of the instances cited in the evidence appeared to be
minor, but no doubt irritating, examples of police
officers `pushing their weight around`, and some of these
had been interpreted as manifestations of racial prejudice
when the officers may well have behaved in a similar way
with white people. It should be remembered that the
police tend to experience the greatest friction with young
people in general, and on many occasions it may be the age
of the person rather than their race which influences the
police officer's behaviour towards them.

An example of the sort of treatment by the police
which can lead to considerable ill-feeling occurred in
1982. On his sixteenth birthday Mark Bravo, a black youth
in north London, bought a motor cycle. During the first
week he was stopped by the police on 7 occasions and this
began a pattern which continued for several months. His
mother kept a record of his encounters during a two-week
period in April 1982: 2 April: stopped 4 times; 4 April:
stopped once; 5 April: stopped twice; 7 April: stopped 7
times; 8 April: stopped twice; 9 April: stopped twice; 14
April: stopped 5 times. Mr. Bravo eventually received 18
summonses as a result of countless stops between January
and the summer; he was acquitted of 10 and those for which
he was found guilty included a `defective registration
plate` which contained a crack (£2 fine), careless driving
(endorsements), and `dangerous part` (£10 fine and
endorsement).92 Of course, every case is distinctive and

40

perhaps there were good reasons for the police to stop this person so often; however in local lore it no doubt goes down as another example of police harassment.

Some police conduct which has led to resentment and anger has been fairly widely reported. For instance, a succession of raids has taken place at the Mangrove Restaurant in Notting Hill. The first occurred in February 1969 and subsequent raids, and resultant charges, such as that against the owner for serving food after 11 p.m., have led to considerable unrest in the area.[93] Raids on the Mangrove continued through the 1970s and into the 1980s, and a particularly notable operation, involving a large number of police officers, occurred on Christmas Eve 1981, just one month after Lord Scarman's report was published in which he called for better relations betwen police and black people.

Railton Road raid:
`institutional disregard for the niceties of the law´

A spectacular police operation took place in Railton Road, Brixton, shortly after the end of the first phase of the Scarman inquiry, and this too prompted a bitter and angry reaction. On 15 July 1981 at 2 a.m. eleven houses were raided by 176 police officers with a further 391 held in reserve. The police had obtained warrants to look for evidence of unlawful drinking under section 187 of the Licensing Act 1964, and to search five houses for petrol bombs under section 6 of the Criminal Damages Act 1971. No evidence of either was found and, indeed, two of the houses for which warrants were granted as a result of `police observations´ turned out to be derelict and unoccupied. The next day pictures were seen, in the press and on television, of wreckage and destruction in the houses - of smashed windows, sinks, toilets, floorboards, furniture, televisions and possessions. Lord Scarman

41

visited the scene of the havoc surrounded by visibly upset
residents, and John Frazer the local Member of Parliament
stated

> I could come to no conclusion other than that a
> large number of policemen had deliberately set
> out to wreck the houses, to make them
> uninhabitable, by taking up floorboards,
> breaking water pipes, removing gas and electric
> meters, hand rails and bannisters and smashing
> almost every window.94

The resultant outcry led to an internal inquiry by
Deputy Assistant Dear (now Chief Constable of the West
Midlands) which exonerated those involved and explained
that police officers had been issued with sledgehammers
and crowbars `to effect speedy entry´. Compensation of
£8,500 was paid by the Metropolitan Police for structural
damage and further sums for damage to personal property,
but as Lord Scarman commented, `compensation is no
substitute for destroyed property´.

Not surprisingly, several formal complaints were
lodged about the police behaviour. However, the Director
of Public Prosecutions decided to take no action. Most
people thought that was the end of the story but, for the
first time ever, the Police Complaints Board resolved to
carry out an investigation under section 8(2) of the
Police Act 1976 which empowered them to report to the Home
Secretary on matters to which his attention should be
drawn `by reason of their gravity or of any other
exceptional circumstances´. The Home Office tried to keep
the report´s existence secret and it only came to light
because of a one-line mention in the Complaints Board´s
Annual Report. Only after pressure in Parliament was a
copy of the special report placed in the House of Commons
Library and in it the Board stated that the Railton Road
raid had involved `serious lapses from professional
standards´ and there had been an `institutional disregard
for the niceties of the law´. The Board also stated that
they were `disappointed´ with the response to their
criticisms by the Deputy Commissioner and they considered

that 'the unprofessional conduct of officers engaged on that operation could be a reflection of their conduct on less sensitive occasions'.[95]

There seems no reason to suppose that the handling of the complaints in the case of the Railton Road raid will have increased public confidence in general, and that of black people in particular, in the way in which complaints are investigated. A common view of the procedure appears to be that there is little point in using it. The British Crime Survey found that less than one person in ten who say they have been annoyed by the police actually make a complaint; 38 per cent of these considered 'it would be no use', 18 per cent thought they might get into trouble and 10 per cent said they are afraid of the consequences.[96] A survey carried out for the Police Federation by MORI in February 1984 revealed a low level of satisfaction with the procedure: 66 per cent said that complaints should be investigated by a body other than the police.

The evidence from the Police Complaints Board shows that the vast majority of complaints are not substantiated. During 1983, for example, the Board completed action on 7,199 complaints cases, containing a total of 16,231 matters of complaint; of these 1,346 (8.3 per cent) resulted in 'advice' to the officers concerned, and a further 234 (1.4 per cent) entailed disciplinary charges.[97] A study by Stevens and Willis showed that the proportion of complainants who were Afro-Caribbean or Asian increased sharply between 1975 and 1976 and thereafter. Furthermore, the study found that whereas the substantiation rate for Asian complainants, in the Metropolitan Police District in the first quarter of 1979, was similar to that of whites (Asians: 2 cases substantiated out of 94 lodged; whites: 53 out of 1716), the substantiation rate for Afro-Caribbeans was much lower: 3 out of 283 complaints.[98] The research showed that Afro-Caribbean complainants were more likely to make complaints of assault, but, in general, serious accusations such as assault are very unlikely to be found proven and a complaint of assault by an Afro-Caribbean or Asian which is substantiated is `rare`, and `very rare` if the complainant is under arrest.

5. A GROWING LACK OF CONFIDENCE

There is little doubt that relations between black people and the police have in general deteriorated, at particularly in London, and the increased number of complaints from members of the ethnic minorities is testimony to the decline. As the evidence presented to the 1971-72 Select Committee showed, in many areas relations were a cause for concern at the beginning of the 1970s, and this is confirmed by other studies.[99] Since then a number of accounts have documented the further deterioration in the confidence which black people have in the police.[100] The Policy Studies Institute report found that whereas 26 per cent of whites felt that some groups `do not get fair treatment´ from the police, 36 per cent of Asians and 62 per cent of West Indians agreed with this view. The research also showed that a much higher proportion of West Indians than of whites or Asians are critical of police conduct, but a lower proportion of West Indians (79 per cent) than of other groups (some 90 per cent) said they would make an official complaint if they felt seriously dissatisfied with the police. The report concluded that:

> These findings suggest that between one-third
> and one-half of West Indians completely lack
> confidence in the police force, and that
> two-thirds have at least considerable doubts
> about standards of police conduct.101

Policing and racial attacks

The attitudes of Asian people towards the police appear to be more favourable than those of Afro-Caribbeans, but they are particularly critical of

45

police behaviour in respect of racial attacks. They complain that police refuse to take calls for assistance seriously, and that they do not charge assailants. The appalling extent of racial attacks has been documented in a number of studies, and it is clear that assaults on members of the ethnic minorities are now all too common in some city areas, particularly in parts of London. The incidence of unprovoked attacks, especially on Asian people, appears to have increased considerably since 1976. During this period Asian shops have been attacked, Asians' houses damaged and burned and a number of Asian people murdered. Peter Fryer reports that 31 black people were murdered by racists between 1976 and 1981, and a report by the Bethnal Green and Stepney Trades Council documented over one hundred racial attacks between 1976 and 1978 in Tower Hamlets alone.[102] The report showed that racial abuse and attacks were common and particularly suffered by Bengalis, who frequently expressed little confidence in the police. Indeed, it was suggested that often the police appeared more concerned with whether the victim was an illegal immigrant than with apprehending and prosecuting the assailants.

It was evident that the National Front was actively encouraging racial hostility in many of the areas where attacks were occurring, even if its direct involvement in them was hard to prove. When, during the election campaign in 1979, the National Front provocatively decided to hold a meeting in Southall, it was not surprising that local people and the Anti-Nazi League responded to the challenge. On 23 April 1979, about 3,000 people demonstrated against the meeting and 2,756 police officers were present to keep public order. However, at the end of the day - `a day dedicated to peaceful protest against the provocation of an alien racist presence' - hundreds of demonstrators and police were injured, 345 people were arrested and Blair Peach was dead.[103]

Eye witness reports, from a wide variety of
sources, testified to examples of police
behaviour to effect arrests or disperse crowds
which ranged from the unreasonable to the
downright brutal.104

All the accounts of the `Battle of Southall´ seem to
agree that the police response was ferocious and included
racial abuse. The Daily Telegraph, for example, described
how the police `cornered about 50 demonstrators´ and then

several dozen, crying, screaming coloured
demonstrators were dragged...to the police
station and waiting coaches. Nearly every
demonstrator we saw had blood flowing from some
sort of injury; some were doubled up in pain.105

The police claim that they merely responded to attacks by
some of the protestors, but other accounts suggest that
police conduct was largely to blame, and that the Special
Patrol Group in particular meted out violence
indiscriminately. There seems little doubt that the
police behaviour, `left a deep scar on the people of
Southall which will take years to heal´.106

Southall was the worst in a series of confrontations
at places such as Lewisham, Tameside, Leicester, Coventry
and elsewhere. The vision of large numbers of police
protecting gatherings of people shouting racial abuse and
inciting racial hatred did little to foster improved
relations between the police and the black communities,
and when police officers themselves used racial insults
and appeared to attack anti-racist demonstrators
indiscriminately, further damage to these relations was
caused.

Racial attacks and harassment have continued to
increase during recent years in a number of areas. These
have been documented in various reports such as those by
the Home Office in 1981, the Runnymede Trust a year later
and the Greater London Council in 1984.107 The GLC Report
detailed a number of horrifying incidents and was
particularly critical of police response. Evidence showed

47

that the police were `deeply implicated in London´s racial harassment problems´ and `officers were alleged to be hostile to or disinterested in the experiences of black victims´.

> The result of these abuses is that London´s police are viewed by many blacks with fear, suspicion and hostility. They are seen, not only as potential perpetrators of racial harassment, but also as sympathetic to the individuals and groups who continue to carry out harassment unchecked by the law.108

It is clearly an overstatement to suggest that the police in general are indifferent to serious crime suffered by numbers of the ethnic minority population, but, as the detailed case studies reveal, a significant number of police officers have failed to deal properly with many incidents. Whether this is out of a misguided belief that good race relations are best fostered by pretending there is no problem, or whether it is caused by racist views, or by lazy officers, is a matter of debate. There is little doubt, though, that a few celebrated cases in which the police have appeared to take tough action against people who are seeking to defend themselves, rather than against their attackers, have led to widespread cynicism about policing policies among many members of the ethnic minorities.

In Bradford twelve Asian youths were charged with very serious offences of conspiracy, but they successfully argued that they had acted in self-defence. The Home Office report on racial violence revealed that there was considerable evidence of such attacks in the city, but police officers involved in the case of the `Bradford Twelve´ in 1982 seemed not even to be aware of the report´s existence. In another well-known case, many people believed that the fire at 439 New Cross Road in OrDeptford on 18 January 1981, which led to the deaths of 13 young black people and the injury of some 30 others, was caused by a racial attack. The police gave a high priority to the investigation but the cause of the fire has never been publicly established. It is clear from the Policy Studies Institute report that the senior police officers decided early in their enquiries that it was _not_ caused by an attack from outside and they expected hostility and lack of co-operation from black witnesses. The researchers stress

> the widespread damage caused to relations between the police and black people in London by the repercussions of the fire.109

Another significant case came to court on 17 November 1983. Eight young Asian men were accused of various offences including affray, assault and possession of offensive weapons, and until withdrawn a few weeks before the Old Bailey trial all the defendants had been also charged with conspiracy. The prosecution alleged that on 24 September 1982 three plain clothes policemen had been attacked by a gang, including the accused. However, a number of significant inconsistencies were apparent in the police evidence and independent witnesses corroborated the defendants´ account that they were peacefully accompanying children on their way home from school. It emerged that the children had been subject to threats, and asaults by skinheads, and each of the defendants had been the victim of at least one racial attack. The defence alleged that the three police officers in plain clothes had attacked the group after comments such as `OK Paki bastard, let´s see what you´re made of´. Allegations of abuse and assaults during the journey to the police station, and while the defendants were in custody, were denied by the police.

During the five-week trial many accounts were given of racial attacks and harassment in Newham and elsewhere, and a lack of police interest and help. The Guardian reported that the Old Bailey jury heard how

> Asian families in the East End of London lived a nightmarish existence of abuse and attacks from white racialists...

Mr. Kulwant Singh Mangat, general secretary of the Sikh Temple in Newham stated that his community had little faith in the police, and the court heard of

Asian homes which were constantly boarded up to protect their occupants from stone-throwing gangs, and of temples and schools where Asian youths had to mount patrols to deter racialist attackers.110

It was suggested that not only did the police fail to protect the Asian people, but they often threatened the victims with prosecution, or indeed charged them, when they sought to defend themselves. In court local police said they had never heard of the Home Office report on racial attacks and indeed denied being aware of any racially-motivated attacks in the Newham area. Four of the `Newham Eight´ were acquitted, while the other four were each sentenced to 50 hours community service for the crimes of affray, and in the case of one, for common assault. In May 1985 another Old Bailey trial opened, this time of the `Newham Seven´ - again young Asians variously accused of affray, assault, possession of offensive weapons and criminal damage. A catalogue or racial attacks and alleged police indifference was revealed, and the defence case of `self defence: no offence´ was largely upheld by the verdicts on 10 July 1985.

Sir Kenneth Newman, Metropolitan Police Commissioner, announced in his January 1985 report to the Home Secretary that he was adding racial attacks to his target areas for special attention which also include robbery, burglary, autocrime, drug abuse and vandalism.111 It remains to be seen how effective the targetting will be, but press and television reports in 1985 and early 1986 suggested that the problem, in parts of London at least, is steadily growing worse.112 On 13 July 1985, in Ilford, London, a particularly horrifying

Mr. Kulwant Singh Mangat, general secretary of the Sikh Temple in Newham stated that his community had little faith in the police, and the court heard of

> Asian homes which were constantly boarded up to protect their occupants from stone-throwing gangs, and of temples and schools where Asian youths had to mount patrols to deter racialist attackers.110

It was suggested that not only did the police fail to protect the Asian people, but they often threatened the victims with prosecution, or indeed charged them, when they sought to defend themselves. In court local police said they had never heard of the Home Office report on racial attacks and indeed denied being aware of any racially-motivated attacks in the Newham area. Four of the `Newham Eight´ were acquitted, while the other four were each sentenced to 50 hours community service for the crimes of affray, and in the case of one, for common assault. In May 1985 another Old Bailey trial opened, this time of the `Newham Seven´ - again young Asians variously accused of affray, assault, possession of offensive weapons and criminal damage. A catalogue or racial attacks and alleged police indifference was revealed, and the defence case of `self defence: no offence´ was largely upheld by the verdicts on 10 July 1985.

Sir Kenneth Newman, Metropolitan Police Commissioner, announced in his January 1985 report to the Home Secretary that he was adding racial attacks to his target areas for special attention which also include robbery, burglary, autocrime, drug abuse and vandalism.111 It remains to be seen how effective the targetting will be, but press and television reports in 1985 and early 1986 suggested that the problem, in parts of London at least, is steadily growing worse.112 On 13 July 1985, in Ilford, London, a particularly horrifying

Eye witness reports, from a wide variety of sources, testified to examples of police behaviour to effect arrests or disperse crowds which ranged from the unreasonable to the downright brutal.104

All the accounts of the `Battle of Southall´ seem to agree that the police response was ferocious and included racial abuse. The Daily Telegraph, for example, described how the police `cornered about 50 demonstrators´ and then

> several dozen, crying, screaming coloured demonstrators were dragged...to the police station and waiting coaches. Nearly every demonstrator we saw had blood flowing from some sort of injury; some were doubled up in pain.105

The police claim that they merely responded to attacks by some of the protestors, but other accounts suggest that police conduct was largely to blame, and that the Special Patrol Group in particular meted out violence indiscriminately. There seems little doubt that the police behaviour, `left a deep scar on the people of Southall which will take years to heal´.106

Southall was the worst in a series of confrontations at places such as Lewisham, Tameside, Leicester, Coventry and elsewhere. The vision of large numbers of police protecting gatherings of people shouting racial abuse and inciting racial hatred did little to foster improved relations between the police and the black communities, and when police officers themselves used racial insults and appeared to attack anti-racist demonstrators indiscriminately, further damage to these relations was caused.

Racial attacks and harassment have continued to increase during recent years in a number of areas. These have been documented in various reports such as those by the Home Office in 1981, the Runnymede Trust a year later and the Greater London Council in 1984.107 The GLC Report detailed a number of horrifying incidents and was particularly critical of police response. Evidence showed that the police were `deeply implicated in London´s racial harassment problems´ and `officers were alleged to be hostile to or disinterested in the experiences of black victims´.

> The result of these abuses is that London´s police are viewed by many blacks with fear, suspicion and hostility. They are seen, not only as potential perpetrators of racial harassment, but also as sympathetic to the individuals and groups who continue to carry out harassment unchecked by the law.108

It is clearly an overstatement to suggest that the police in general are indifferent to serious crime suffered by numbers of the ethnic minority population, but, as the detailed case studies reveal, a significant number of police officers have failed to deal properly with many incidents. Whether this is out of a misguided belief that good race relations are best fostered by pretending there is no problem, or whether it is caused by racist views, or by lazy officers, is a matter of debate. There is little doubt, though, that a few celebrated cases in which the police have appeared to take tough action against people who are seeking to defend themselves, rather than against their attackers, have led to widespread cynicism about policing policies among many members of the ethnic minorities.

In Bradford twelve Asian youths were charged with very serious offences of conspiracy, but they successfully argued that they had acted in self-defence. The Home Office report on racial violence revealed that there was considerable evidence of such attacks in the city, but police officers involved in the case of the `Bradford Twelve´ in 1982 seemed not even to be aware of the report´s existence. In another well-known case, many people believed that the fire at 439 New Cross Road in OrDeptford on 18 January 1981, which led to the deaths of 13 young black people and the injury of some 30 others, was caused by a racial attack. The police gave a high priority to the investigation but the cause of the fire

48

has never been publicly established. It is clear from the Policy Studies Institute report that the senior police officers decided early in their enquiries that it was <u>not</u> caused by an attack from outside and they expected hostility and lack of co-operation from black witnesses. The researchers stress

> the widespread damage caused to relations between the police and black people in London by the repercussions of the fire.109

Another significant case came to court on 17 November 1983. Eight young Asian men were accused of various offences including affray, assault and possession of offensive weapons, and until withdrawn a few weeks before the Old Bailey trial all the defendants had been also charged with conspiracy. The prosecution alleged that on 24 September 1982 three plain clothes policemen had been attacked by a gang, including the accused. However, a number of significant inconsistencies were apparent in the police evidence and independent witnesses corroborated the defendants´ account that they were peacefully accompanying children on their way home from school. It emerged that the children had been subject to threats, and asaults by skinheads, and each of the defendants had been the victim of at least one racial attack. The defence alleged that the three police officers in plain clothes had attacked the group after comments such as `OK Paki bastard, let´s see what you´re made of´. Allegations of abuse and assaults during the journey to the police station, and while the defendants were in custody, were denied by the police.

During the five-week trial many accounts were given of racial attacks and harassment in Newham and elsewhere and a lack of police interest and help. <u>The Guardian</u> reported that the Old Bailey jury heard how

> Asian families in the East End of London lived a nightmarish existence of abuse and attacks from white racialists...

49

arson attack occurred in which Mrs. Shamira Kassam, who
was eight months pregnant, and her three young children,
were murdered.

A complaint which a number of Asian people have made
is that when they called for police assistance the
officers asked to see their passports and suspected them
of being illegal immigrants. It is alleged, for example,
that Mr. A. apprehended a burglar in his flat in
Lewisham, but when the police arrived they released the
criminal and informed Mr. A that he was not entitled to
council accommodation and then arrested him on suspicion
of being an illegal immigrant. After several hours in
detention he was released without charges.[113] Gordon has
documented a large number of passport raids carried out
since the Immigration Act 1971 and the subsequent
establishment of the Illegal Immigration Intelligence
Unit at Scotland Yard.[114] The scale of these operations,
and the way they have been carried out, have provoked
considerable anger amongst ethnic minority communities.
Recent cases include police raids on sixty Asian homes in
Luton in January 1984, and on Kashmiri homes in
Birmingham two months later. Each raid provokes
hostility amongst the people who experience it and
further alienates members of the ethnic minorities from
the police.

The attitudes of the ethnic minorities

The Policy Studies Institute investigation of the
British black population, which entailed a survey of 5001
adult people, confirmed that the ethnic minorities lack
confidence in the police. In answer to the question `are
people of Asian/West Indian origin treated the same,
better or worse than white people by the police?´, 30 per
cent of Asians said `worse´ and 26 per cent didn´t know.
The belief that the police discriminate against them is

51

far more widespread among Asians than the belief that any other institutions do so, such as the courts, schools, trade unions, pubs, building societies, banks, estate agents and even council housing departments, the only exception being employers. Among West Indians the findings are overwhelming: <u>64 per cent believe that they are treated `worse' than whites by the police,</u> with just 16 per cent saying `the same'; 19 per cent didn't know. Again, far more say that they are discriminated against by the police than by any other institutions.[115]

The survey also revealed that many black people felt that the incidence of racial abuse and attacks had increased during the previous five years and a large number did not believe that they could rely on the police to protect them. 43 per cent of West Indian and 52 per cent of Asian men considered that the problem of racial attacks had worsened (about 20 per cent didn't know), while 42 per cent of Asian men, and 64 per cent of West Indian, men believed that it was `probably' or `definitely' <u>not</u> true that black people could rely on the police for protection. About half the Asians and West Indians believed that black people should organise self-defence groups if necessary to protect themselves from racialist violence. Colin Brown concluded that the data

> show that there is among black people an alarmingly low level of confidence in the support from the police against racial attacks...116

It is clear that relations between many black people and the police are poor, and are characterised by hostility, resentment and lack of confidence. This is particularly evident among young Afro-Caribbean people where there is a `disastrous lack of confidence',[117] but it is also widespread amongst older black people. The evidence presented and reviewed in this paper shows that the crisis of confidence which Lord Scarman found in

52

Brixton exists in various parts of London and other English cities. The data show that black people are stopped and searched, and arrested, far more frequently than other people, and were far more likely to be charged with being a `suspected person´ before the relevant section of the Vagrancy Act 1824 was repealed. Many young black people feel they have been `hunted irrespective of their innocence or guilt´.[118] There are also numerous allegations of racial abuse, harassment and assault by the police, but only a few of these, such as the case of the Whites, have ever been proved. Although the number of formal complaints against the police has risen, few of these are substantiated either.

The depth of hostility and distrust among many black people is more considerable than senior police officers and certain politicians may realise, but possibly not as great as some others have argued. The Policy Studies Institute investigation found that black people are just as likely as white people to report crimes to the police, and even young Afro-Caribbean people, who are the most markedly hostile, do not wholly reject the present policing system. The point of view of many black people was expressed with some poignancy by Derek Humphry, at the beginning of his account of police misbehaviour:

> I am critical of the police force in this book because I wish to respect it... The rule of law in Britain should be a rule which is firm and just (and seen to be such) to peoples of all colours, appearances and incomes.[119]

Unfortunately many black people say that police treatment of members of the ethnic minority communities is not just and, as this paper has tried to show, there is considerable evidence to support them.

6. THREE PARTICULAR PROBLEMS

During a period of rapid change and increased inequalities, disadvantage and unemployment, it is not surprising that the police, as important agents of social control, should experience greater pressures and criticisms. Some of the central problems were examined by the Royal Commission on Criminal Procedure which reported in January 1981[120] and others were highlighted by Lord Scarman in his report ten months later. These inquiries placed a number of issues on the political agenda and after considerable debate the main result was the rather inadequate Police and Criminal Evidence Act 1984, which seems likely to prove irksome, bureaucratic and costly for the police and ineffective in terms of providing an improved service, and safeguards against abuses, for the public.[121]

The legislation does not seem likely to lead to an improvement in relations between black people and the police although, on Lord Scarman's initiative, Section 101 of the Act does make racially discriminatory behaviour a specific police disciplinary offence. From the evidence reviewed in this paper and accounts elsewhere, it seems possible to identify three particular problems which may directly affect race and policing: first, racially prejudiced and discriminatory behaviour, second, officers attitudes and conduct in general, and third, 'institutional racism'.

Racially prejudiced and discriminatory behaviour
by police officers

There is now considerable evidence of racial prejudice among police officers. In addition to that which has been cited, Robert Reiner, for example, reported that a large minority of his sample of police officers volunteered racialist, hostile or suspicious views of black people.[122] Research in Chapeltown, Leeds, in early 1981 found common criticism of ethnic minorities by police, and a general stereotyped view of Asians as no great problem, but liars if suspected of wrong-doing. `West Indians were seen as lazy, easygoing and simple people´ and young blacks were seen as troublesome, disrespectful and uncooperative, and they were considered to be disorderly. The study also reported the common use within the station of racially offensive language.[123] This was dramatically illustrated at the 1984 Police Federation Conference when Peter Johnson, speaking from the platform, referred to `our coloured brethren or nig nogs´. The Federation Chairman, Leslie Curtis, immediately repudiated the remark and Mr. Johnson apologised for his `slip of the tongue´ but, after extensive publicity, he felt obliged to resign from the police service.[124]

The Policy Studies Institute research also found that `racialist language and racial prejudice were prominent and pervasive´. One view put forward to the researchers was

> I freely admit that I hate, loathe and despise niggers. I can´t stand them. I don´t let it affect my job though. There are some decent ones, though, like that bloke we´ve just dealt with.[125]

The study suggested that the remark may accurately reflect experience, in that prejudice does not invariably result in discriminatory behaviour.

The argument has been put many times that police prejudice reflects that in society, but there cannot be many occupational groups, which regard themselves as respectable professionals, in which racialist talk is as pervasive as it is reported to be within the police. The West Midlands Chief Constable, Sir Philip Knights, who retired in 1985, said that racialist police officers existed, but probably no more than in the community as a whole; however, Lord Scarman stressed `we cannot rest on the cynical proposition, which I have heard, that, since the police will necessarily reflect social attitudes, racially prejudiced people are bound to be found in their ranks´.[126]

As a result of the Scarman report, the Police Training Council recommended in 1983 that `racism awareness training´ should be introduced, and initially four pilot schemes were established. The reaction to these has not been uncritical from within the police service and from outside, but it seems likely that increased emphasis will be placed on training in this area.[127] As well as the inclusion of racially prejudiced behaviour as a specific offence in the Police Discipline Code, Lord Scarman also recommended that concerted attempts should be made to prevent the recruitment of racialists by the police. Research by Colman and Gorman of the University of Leicester did reveal that `conservative and authoritarian personalities´ appeared to be particularly attracted to the police service, and their small sample of recruits showed hostility to black people. Essays by police cadets at the Peel Centre, Hendon, extracts from which were published in newspapers in 1982, revealed some extreme examples of prejudice and racial hatred.[128] Certainly it would seem reasonable to expect that tests could be applied which would prevent people with such violent views becoming police officers, although it would be less easy to preclude the recruitment of people who are more insidiously racialist.

Lord Scarman was also concerned to increase the number of police officers recruited from the ethnic minorities. He found that in the whole of England and Wales in October 1981 there were only 326 black officers, a mere 0.3 per cent of the total; by late 1985 this had risen to 726. Evidence from the Policy Studies Institute research, and from a recent article in Policing, suggests that black police officers experience prejudice from their colleagues, and in their dealings with white and black members of the public, and have little if any effect on the pervasive racialist talk within the police.[129] There continues to be considerable difficulty in attracting more applicants from the ethnic minorities.

Police officers' relations with the public and the `offence´ of `contempt of cop´

It seems quite plausible that some police behaviour which is interpreted as racial discrimination or harassment by black people is not that as such but rather `heavy-handed´ or discourteous conduct by police officers, not prompted by racial motives. It should be stressed that studies, surveys and opinion polls consistently tend to show that the public have a reasonably high opinion of the police. The first British Crime Survey, for example, revealed that three out of four people considered the police did a `very good´ or `fairly good´ job in their area, and four out of five people who had come into contact with the police in the recent past said they had been helpful and pleasant.[130]

The Policy Studies Institute survey also found that a majority of people who had encountered a police officer commented favourably on his or her attitude, although the figures varied from 79 per cent for white people, to 64 per cent for Asians and 60 per cent for West Indians. The PSI survey asked a number of questions on police success and found that public confidence varied considerably, depending on which aspect of policing was being assessed. For example, 80 per cent thought that the police were `very successful´ or `fairly successful´ at coping with marches and demonstrations but only 31 per cent expressed these opinions about curbing domestic burglaries. Seven out of ten people thought the police were successful at `getting on with people´ but only 43 per cent of black people expressed this view.[131]

The British Crime Survey showed that members of the public who approach the police have markedly varying opinions about them. Older people were more satisfied than younger, women more than men, non-manual workers more than manual, and those living in rural areas more than those in towns. `Only one in five young men in inner cities felt that the police had been "very pleasant", as opposed to four out of five elderly women in rural areas´.[132] Of those who had been approached by the police, 52 per cent of young men said that they had received impolite treatment, and over a third aged between 16 and 24, said they had been annoyed.

Contacts between police officers and young people seem to be far from satisfactory. This is particularly evident in the case of young black people, as the PSI study found and as Southgate´s research in Chapeltown revealed. Here, police officers complained that young black people would not respond as co-operatively and respectfully as young whites, while young West Indians resented the formality of police officers. Southgate also noted that older officers criticised the ability of younger ones to get on well with the public in general.[133] A high proportion of police constables are young - in England and Wales in 1980 some 36 per cent were aged between 18 and 25 - and it has been argued that they lack the experience and maturity to handle difficult encounters effectively and reasonably amiably.

Lord Scarman drew attention to the importance of proper guidance and supervision for young police officers `in discharging their difficult, delicate and indispensable function´ and he advocated improved monitoring and management of constables on the streets to minimise misconduct.[134] However it is not clear that his recommendations have been virorously acted upon, and indeed there are considerable difficulties in achieving satisfactory supervision. Police officers are given great discretion in the way they carry out their duties, and much depends upon the attitudes of individual officers and the people they encounter. The expectations and stereotypes of both police officers and members of the public are important in determining how incidents are revolved. This seems to be particularly significant in contacts betwen young officers and young people, and especially young black people. If their attitudes are hostile, abrasive and disrespectful the result may be an arrest for `contempt of cop´.[135]

Institutionalised discrimination: the problem of `institutional racism´

It has been argued by many people that the prejudice and misconduct of individual officers are not the only reasons for `racist policing´: a prime cause is `institutional racism´. There is some difficulty about this concept for it seems to be used in the debate about race, crime and policing in at least four different ways. First it is argued that the policies of the police service are intentionally racially discriminatory while second it is claimed they are unintentionally so. The third usage applies the concept to society in general and to government policies and agencies in particular and argues that some of these are deliberately racist while the fourth way in which it is used is similar but suggests that the racist outcomes may be unintentional.[136]

There is some evidence to support each contention. A number of people have argued that immigration policies are intentionally racially discriminatory and, in fact, they are. The various acts to control immigration, and particularly the concept of `patriality', have been specifically designed to prevent the entry of Afro-Caribbean and Asian people. `Immigration law defined the presence of black people - not white racism - as the problem'.[137] Others, while not denying the intentional racism of Home Office policies on immigration and deportation, have pointed out that institutionalised racism is more insidious; Salman Rushdie stated that

> 400 years of conquest and looting, centuries of being told that you are superior to the fuzzy-wuzzies and the wogs, leave their stain on you all; such a stain seeps into every part of your culture, your language and your daily life; and nothing much has been done to wash it out.[138]

As Rex has explained `racism is something which pertains not simply to the psychology of individuals but to the belief systems which operate in society'.[139] Certain institutions may amplify this racism through sub-cultures, and this seems evident in the police - thus the `prominent and pervasive' racialism discovered in the Metropolitan Police by the Policy Studies Institute researchers.

Lord Scarman rejected the general allegation that Britain `is a society which knowingly, as a matter of policy, discriminates against black people' and he `totally and unequivocally' repudiated the accusation that the direction and policies of the Metropolitan Police are racist.[140] However, evidence cited in this review demonstrates that, at the very least, the outcomes of the institution's policies are racially discriminatory - witness the number of black people stopped and searched, and arrested. One must also query why Scotland Yard released racially-based crime statistics, knowing that their comprehensiveness and accuracy was open to question and presumably being aware that they would be construed as linking race and crime, or, put more simply, that they would create a popular image of black people as criminals. Hence remarks such as those of Mr. Worsthorne in The Sunday Telegraph of 29 November 1981:

Brixton is the iceberg tip of a crisis of ethnic criminality which is not Britain's fault - except in the sense that her rulers quite unnecessarily imported it.

As Reiner argues, particular targetting of certain crimes or areas by the police can result in institutionalised racism, in the sense of unintentionally discriminating against people on the basis of race; Operation Swamp can be seen as such an example.[141] Research by Landau showed that the police in London appeared to exercise discretion in a biased way in cases involving juveniles. His investigation in five divisions of the Metropolitan Police in 1978-79 entailed the examination of 1,708 cases and he found that black juveniles, in comparable cases and circumstances, were more likely to be treated severely and charged by the police rather than referred to the juvenile bureau.[142] Individual cases might be explained by particular officer's prejudice, or by features of the interaction between specific suspects and police officers dealing with them, such as insolence and disrespect, but the cumulative result, whereby young blacks are treated more harshly, may be seen as another manifestation of institutionalised discrimination.

7. A CONTINUING TALE OF FAILURE?

Race and policing: the wider context

Policing and race cannot be isolated from the wider context within which it takes place. This includes racial discrimination, inner city unemployment, deprivation and crime, and racial disadvantage, which is partly the result of the location of the ethnic minorities but largely a result of past and present discrimination. Another important part of the context is the general change in the style of policing, especially in urban areas, during the last twenty years.

The changes in the style of policing in the last two decades or so have been charted and examined in a number of studies.[143] In an interesting article Robert Reiner considered five associated trends which lead towards a `police state'. These are centralisation, increasing police powers, militarisation, pervasiveness, and de-democratisation; Reiner concluded that `each is undoubtedly occurring in Britain, to some extent, now', but he stressed that there are also a number of counter-tendencies.[144]

Unlike many countries, Britain does not have a national police force under one unified command, but many fear that there is a trend in this direction. The National Reporting Centre, which was established in 1972 and was prominent during the 1984-85 coal dispute, is claimed by some to be evidence of the trend of centralisation, although perhaps more convincing is the reduction in the number of forces from 126 before 1964 to the present 43. The importance of chief constables has grown apace during this period, accompanied by a decline in the influence of local police committees. Perhaps the most significant change in policing is that it seems to have become remote from people. The advent of panda cars, and the consequent removal of many foot patrols, was an important factor in distancing the police, and so too was the establishment of a number of large police forces in the aftermath of the 1964 Act.

Police officers have also seemed to be increasingly prepared to take part in political debate and this may have undermined the previous impression of impartiality. The Police Federation has organised a number of campaigns, notably on the restoration of the death penalty, and the Federation's parliamentary spokesman regularly pontificates in the media on all sorts of social questions. Sir Robert Mark was in the forefront of the politicisation of the police service when, during his period as Metropolitan Police Commissioner, he made a series of attacks on politicians and parts of the criminal justice system, such as juries.[145] Other chief officers have had much to say about politics and society; James Anderton, for instance, Chief Constable of Greater Manchester, remarked in 1982, `I firmly believe that there is a long-term political strategy to destroy the proven structures of the police and turn them into an exclusive agency of a one-party state.'[146]

In 1985, Mr. Anderton was again warning the Association of Chief Police Officers not to become `the willing instrument of unscrupulous politicians', and he pointed out too that crime had never been so extensive and he had never known so many demands on the police, and indeed at times he felt `quite helpless'.[147] He did not point out that there have never been more police officers: the total rose by 12,000 between 1979 and 1985 and expenditure by 154 per cent.

63

The image of policing also seems to have changed considerably during the last twenty years. Within the service specialisation and `results´, in terms of successful arrests, are seen as means to promotion and this is arguably at the expense of the helpful, service role of officers on the beat. Police officers are frequently seen rushing around in fast cars, or involved in public order operations which are violent. The image of the friendly but firm George Dixon, who knew his `patch´ and the people living there, has given way to the `fire-brigade´ policing of The Sweeney and The Bill. The changed image of policing, and its politicisation, may help to explain the beleaguered and defensive attitudes of many officers who deeply resent criticisms such as those reviewed earlier.

These factors must be considered alongside the increased centralisation and specialisation, and the belief in professionalism. The police `run the risk of becoming, by reason of their professionalism, a "corps d´elite" set apart from the rest of the community´, said Lord Scarman, and he advocated consultation and accountability to prevent `them from slipping into an enclosed fortress of inward thinking and social isolation which would in the long term result in a siege mentality´.[148] Some have argued that this position has been reached in parts of Britain´s inner cities, and that the police feel isolated from hostile and resentful sections of the communities, which in turn view the police as remote and threatening.

The nostalgic view of a `golden age´ of policing in the 1950s and 1960s is clearly an over-simplification, as Basil Griffiths stressed: `there exists and has existed since the days of the industrial revolution hard core urban areas where a positive hatred is maintained towards the police by a sizeable minority of the people´.[149]

Inner city areas have never been easy to police, for it is
here that crime is highest, poverty and poor housing the
most widespread and unemployment a major affliction:

> Police working in the inner city are under
> constant stress of a degree that would drive
> most people to the verge of nervous breakdown.
> They would not be human if they did not on
> occasion over-react.150

Race and policing: the spiral of decline

Conditions in many of Britain's inner city areas are
appalling for many of the inhabitants. It is no wonder
that the simmering cauldron occasionally boils over in an
outburst of anger and bitterness, and it is no surprise
that the police should be the targets for this violence.
They are the visible symbols of a government which is
allowing these areas to decline alarmingly, and they are
the daily enforcers of order. When their conduct is
considered to be unjust, or abusive, or harassing, then
the mixture indeed becomes explosive. Waddington, the
regular polemicist in the Federation's magazine Police,
has nicely put the point about policing the inner cities:

> Here, most of all, what is required is
> impartial, impersonal authority and restrained
> use of force. In these areas the police may
> indeed be seen as a visible irritant. It is
> even more essential, therefore, that they be
> seen as representatives of the law, above
> considerations of class and race.151

Just so, but as the evidence in this paper shows,
many black people in Britain's cities do not believe the
police are impartial or that they are particularly
restrained in their use of force. The hostility and
resentment of many black people means that in some areas
the police receive little co-operation or information and
consequently find it difficult to clear up crime. As a
result, they adopt heavy-handed methods, frequently
employ stop and search powers and sometimes `bend the
rules´ to try to root out criminals and this leads to a

further deterioration in relations with local people and even greater lack of information. This vicious circle or spiral of decline in police relations with local people, often both black and white, is just one of several trends evident in inner cities.[152]

Racial abuse, harassment and discrimination are common in some areas, as this paper shows. These are vital causes of `the crisis of confidence´ which Lord Scarman found in Brixton, and which exists elsewhere. He reported that an account of relations between the police and the public in Brixton was `a tale of failure´ and that must be the judgement in the wider area of race and policing. The spiral of decline in relations between the police and black people could be arrested if appropriate initiatives were firmly implemented, but at present there is little cause for optimism.

Is the tale of failure set to continue?

The depressingly familiar reactions to the 1985 disorders, by Government Ministers, some police officers and most media commentators, suggest that little has been learned from the 1981 riots and Lord Scarman´s report. The view that riots are `alien to our streets´ is a dramatic case of historical amnesia (for an outline of disorder in the 1930s see Appendix B) and the responses that the disorders are `senseless´ crimes caused by agitators, subversives and `wickedness´ lead inexorably to tougher measures to combat `the enemy within´. However, wiser counsellors down the ages have known that while repression may work in the short-term, (although at great cost), it cannot be a lasting solution. As Edmund Burke wrote in 1775:

> The use of force alone is temporary. It may
> subdue for a moment, but it does not remove the
> necessity of subduing again.

The use of CS gas and plastic bullets, the adoption of foreign police tactics to crush disorder and the imposition of more stringent penalties and sanctions will not remove the underlying causes of the riots. Indeed, there is considerable evidence to show that repression leads to an even greater disorder. Gurr has pointed to a strong relationship between an increase in force by a regime and the occurrence of disturbances and Johnson found that repressive measures often lead to a greater potential for collective violence.153

The increased use of coercion is likely to erode many citizens' perceptions of the regime's legitimacy, to undermine the authority of the state and its agents such as the police, and to fuel feelings of injustice. As consent diminishes, non-compliance and `hostile outbursts' increase and so greater coercion is required, leading in turn to less consent. Thus policing and disorder can enter a vicious circle, because the response to the initial rioting fails to tackle the root causes. Is this the route that Britain has chosen to take? There seems to be a failure to appreciate that when people are dispossessed, politically excluded and deprived of hope, they may become frustrated, indignant and angry. If they experience police harassment and abuse, or if they believe that the police are behaving unjustly, they may erupt in fury, although such an outburst is likely to be shortlived and cathartic.

The Government steadfastly refused to hold a public inquiry into the 1985 disorders, preferring to requisition reports by the police forces involved. It seems quite incredible that rioting as serious as that which occurred should not be subject to an inquiry under the Police Act 1964. Indeed, in view of the disorders and the deterioration in relations between many black people and the police, and the increasing politicisation and criticism of the police, there is now an overwhelming case for a Royal Commission on the Police. Unfortunately, under the present administration this course of action looks most unlikely, and instead tougher measures and unconditional support for whatever chief constables decide is the order of the day.

And so the spiral of decline in police relations with local people, black and white, in many inner city areas, which is highlighted in the paper, looks set to continue. Heavy-handed methods, frequent use of stop and search powers, and hard policing in general will cause increased hostility and resentment and a consequent decrease in cooperation and information, making it more difficult to clear up crimes. The police in such areas will feel even more beleaguered and hostile, and the gulf between them and local people, especially the black and the young, will grow even wider. It is to be hoped that this is an unduly pessimistic view and that wiser counsels prevail. However, the portents are not promising. The Government has introduced new legislative measures for controlling public order, which look likely to inflame rather than heal. It is surely no coincidence that the last Public Order Act was passed in 1936, at a time of high unemployment, social deprivation and antagonism between the police and certain sections of the public (See Appendix B), and its successor act is to be passed fifty years later in similar circumstances.

It also seems that some police officers are determined to go on the offensive. This was illustrated graphically at 7am on 30 October 1985 when about 100 officers raided seven houses in Brailsford Road and Arlingford Road in Brixton. The police were looking for property stolen during the riots a month earlier, but none was found. The officers used sledgehammers to break down the doors of the houses, and then took photographs of the occupants. Mr Patrick Highland, aged 74, was photographed as he lay in bed. One resident was quoted as saying `I asked an officer why they hadn't knocked on the door or rung the bell to be let in, rather than smash the door down. He said "It's a form of habit".´ The Chairman of the Community Police Consultative Group for Lambeth described the raids as brutal, irresponsible and provocative, and pointed out that they were carried out without the knowledge of the police community liaison officer.

If determined action was taken the spiral of decline could be reversed. Instead it seems that palliatives are to be applied, which in fact are likely to exacerbate the underlying causes of unrest and disorder. Ghettos are being created, characterised by deprivation and neglect, tough policing and repressive measures and disintegrating political authority and a lack of social cohesion. Is this to be the future story of race and policing? Is the tale of failure set to continue?

1   The author gratefully acknowledges the award of a
     Research Fellowship by The Leverhulme Trust, and
     consequent financial support towards the production
     of this study.

2   The Archbishop of Canterbury's Commission on Urban
     Priority Areas, Faith in the City : A Call for
     Action by Church and Nation, London : Church House,
     1985, para. 14.67, p.351 and para. 14.29, p.339.

3   The Brixton Disorders 10-12 April 1981 : Report of
     an Inquiry by the Rt.Hon. the Lord Scarman, OBE,
     London : HMSO, 1981 (Cmnd. 8427), para. 4.43.

4   Steve Platt, `The innocents of Broadwater Estate',
     New Society, Vol. 74, No. 1189, 11 October 1985, pp.
     48-49.

5   For an account of various reactions to, and
     explanations of, the 1981 disorders see John Benyon,
     `The riots, Lord Scarman and the political agenda'
     and Graham Murdock, `Reporting the riots : images
     and impact' in John Benyon (ed.), Scarman and After:
     Essays reflecting on Lord Scarman's Report, the
     riots and their aftermath, Oxford : Pergamon Press,
     1984, pp. 3-19 and 73-95.

6   The Brixton Disorders, supra note 3, para. 2.38.

7   The Brixton Disorders, para. 3.110, emphasis added.

8   This was Lord Scarman's view, of the 1981 disorders:
     see The Brixton Disorders,   Ch. 6; see also S.
     Field and P. Southgate, Public Disorder, London:
     HMSO, 1982 (Home Office Research Study No.72).

9   The Brixton Disorders, supra note 3, para.4.1.

10   For an account of the area before the riot, which
     predicted that disorder would break out, see Ken
     Pryce, Endless Pressure, Harmondsworth: Penguin,
     1979; see also Martin Kettle and Lucy Hodges,
     Uprising!, London: Pan, 1982, ch.1; Harris Joshua,
     Tina Wallace and Heather Booth, To Ride the Storm:
     The 1981 Bristol `Riot´ and the State, London:
     Heinemann, 1983; Tony Jefferson and Roger Grimshaw,
     Controlling the Constable, London: Muller, 1984,
     pp.78-82.

11   Quotation attributed to the Liverpool 8 Defence
     Committee in The Times, 13 November 1981.

12   Michael Nally, `Eyewitness in Moss Side´, in John
     Benyon (ed.), Scarman and After, Oxford: Pergamon
     Press, 1984, pp.54-62.

13   Home Office, Statistical Bulletin, London: Home
     Office, 1982, Issue 20/82 (13 October 1982) pp.1-9.

14   See for example Derek Humphry, Police Power and
     Black People, London: Panther, 1972; Maureen Cain,
     Society and the Policeman´s Role, London: Routledge
     and Kegan Paul, 1973; J.R. Lambert, Crime, Police
     and Race Relations, London: Oxford University Press,
     1970; R. Moore, Racism and Black Resistance, London:
     Pluto, 1975; Institute of Race Relations, Police
     Against Black People, London: Institute of Race
     Relations, 1979; Stuart Hall et al., Policing the
     Crisis: Mugging, the State and Law and Order,

London: Macmillan, 1978; Paul Gordon, White Law: Racism in the Police, Courts and Prisons, London: Pluto Press, 1983; Chris Mullard, Black Britain, London: Allen and Unwin, 1973;

15   G. Greaves, `The Brixton disorders´, in John Benyon (ed.), Scarman and After, Oxford: Pergamon Press, 1984, p.67.

16   Clare Demuth, `Sus´: a Report on the Vagrancy Act, London: Runnymede Trust, 1978.

17   Philip Stevens and Carole Willis, Race, Crime and Arrests, London: HMSO, 1979 (Home Office Research Study No. 58), pp.31-33.

18   House of Commons, Race Relations and the `Sus´ Law: Second Report from the Home Affairs Committee, Session 1979-80, HC 559, London: HMSO, 1980.

19   Anne Brogden, `"Sus" is dead but what about "Sas"?´, New Community, Vol.9, No.1 (Summer 1981); Merseyside Police Authority, The Merseyside Disturbances: the Role and Responsibility of the Police Authority, Liverpool: Merseyside County Council, 1981; Peter Southgate, `The Disturbances of July 1981 in Handsworth, Birmingham´ in Simon Field and Peter Southgate, Public Dis<rder, London: HMSO, 1982 (Home Office Research Study No. 72) pp.50-51; Mary Tuck and Peter Southgate, Ethnic Minorities, Crime and Policing, London: HMSO, 1981 (Home Office Research Study No.70).

20   Carole Willis, The Use, Effectiveness and Impact of Police Stop and Search Powers, London: Home Office, 1983 (Research and Planning Unit Paper 15).

21   Police and People in London, Vol.1: David J. Smith,
      A Survey of Londoners, London: Policy Studies
      Institute, 1983 (PSI No.618), ch.4, pp.89-154.

22   Ibid., pp. 117-118.

23   The Brixton Disorders, supra note 3, paras.
      4.37-4.40.

24   The Brixton Disorders, para. 4.43 and para. 4.76.

25   Stevens and Willis, Race, Crime and Arrests, supra
      note 17, pp.15-18.

26   Ibid., p.41.

27   For a critical discussion of the Stevens and Willis
      study see John Lea and Jock Young, What is to be
      done about Law and Order?, Harmondsworth: Penguin,
      1984, pp.147-162.

28   Police and People in London, Vol.1: Smith, A Survey
      of Londoners, supra, note 21, pp.118-126.

29   Police and People in London, Vol.3: David J. Smith,
      A Survey of Police Officers, London: Policy Studies
      Institute, 1983 (PSI No.620), pp.88-91.

30   Select Committee on Race Relations and Immigration,
      Session 1976-77, The West Indian Community: Vol.1,
      Report, Vols.2 and 3, Evidence, HC 180, London:
      HMSO, February 1977.

31   Ibid., Vol.2, `Memorandum by the Metropolitan
      Police' (25 March 1976), pp.179-182 and p.188.

32   Ibid., Vol.3 `Memorandum by the Community Relations Commission´ (14 October 1976), pp.529-532 and `Commentary by Professor Morris on the Memorandum by the Metropolitan Police´, pp.548-554.

33   Ibid., Vol.3, `Commentary by Professor Morris....´, p.551.

34   Ibid., Vol.1, Report, p.xxxi, para.103.

35   Select Committee on Race Relations and Immigration, Session 1971-72, Police/Immigrant Relations: Vol. 1, Report, HC 471, London: HMSO, August 1972, p.71, para.242.

36   Ibid., Vol.2, Evidence, Vol.3, Evidence, Documents and Index, HC 471, London: HMSO, August 1972.

37   Lea and Young, What is to be done about Law and Order?, supra note 27, pp.135-138; see also J. Lea and J. Young, `Urban violence and political marginalisation: the riots in Britain, summer 1981´, Critical Social Policy, No.3, 1982; J. Lea and J. Young, `Riots in Britain: alienated cultures´, Chartist, No.87, October/ November 1981; J. Lea and J. Young, `A missed opportunity´, New Socialist, January/February 1982; J. Lea and J. Young, `Race and Crime´, Marxism Today, August 1982.

38   Lea and Young, What is to be done about Law and Order?, supra note 27, p.138.

39   Ibid., pp.165-168.

40   Ibid., p.166.

41   L. Wilkins, Social Deviance Social Policy, Action and Research, London: Tavistock, 1974; J. Young, The Drugtakers, London: MacGibbon and Kee, 1971.

42   Lee Bridges and Paul Gilroy, `Striking back', Marxism Today 1982; see also Lee Bridges, `Policing the urban wasteland', Race and Class, Vol.25, Autumn 1983; Lee Bridges, `Extended views: the British left and law and order', Sage Race Relations Abstracts, February 1983; Paul Gilroy, `The myth of black criminality', Socialist Register 1982, London: Merlin, 1982; Paul Gilroy, `Police and thieves', in Centre for Contemporary Cultural Studies, The Empire Strikes Back, London: Hutchinson, 1983.

43   Stuart Hall, Chas Critcher, Tony Jefferson, John Clarke, Brian Roberts, Policing the Crisis: Mugging, the State and Law and Order, London: Macmillan, 1978, p.338.

44   Ibid., ch.10, `The politics of "mugging"', pp.327-397.

45   Ibid., p.359.

46   `The police and the black wageless', Race Today, February 1972.

47   House of Commons Official Report, Parliamentary Debates (Hansard), Session 1975-76, Fifth Series, Vol.917, 19 October 1976, Written Answers, cols. 368-9.

48   Report of the Commissioner of Police for the Metropolis, London: HMSO, 1964, cited in Hall et al., Policing the Crisis, supra note 43, p.5.

49   The Times, 10 June 1863; The Times, 7 November 1862;
        The Times, 1 December 1862; see Geoffrey Pearson,
        Hooligan: A History of Respectable Fears, London:
        Macmillan, 1983, pp.128-142; see also K. Chesney,
        The Victorian Underworld, Harmondsworth: Penguin,
        1972.

50   Stanley Cohen, Folk Devils and Moral Panics, St.
        Albans: Granada, 1973, p.9.

51   Derek Humphry, `Danger signals from the streets of
        Lambeth´, The Sunday Times, 5 January 1975.

52   See Select Committee on Race Relations and
        Immigration, Session 1976-77, The West Indian
        Community, supra note 30, Vol.2, `Memorandum by the
        Community Relations Commission´ (14 October 1976),
        p.530, para B6; see also Vol.3, Appendix 21,
        `Additional memorandum by the Metropolitan Police´,
        pp.689-696; an abridged version of the confidential
        Brixton study is printed as Annex `A´, pp.696-702.

53   The Times, 13 January 1975; Evening News, 15 January
        1975; Sunday Express, 19 January 1975.

54   Judge Gwynn Morris quoted in the Daily Mail, 16 May
        1975, cited by Hall et al., Policing the Crisis,
        supra note 43, p.333.

55   Quoted in The Guardian, 1 September 1976, cited by
        Paul Gordon, White Law: Racism in the Police, Courts
        and Prisons, London: Pluto Press, 1983, p.41.

56   Select Committee on Race Relations and Immigration, Session 1976-77, _The West Indian Community_, _supra_, note 30, Vol.2, `Memorandum by the Community Relations Commission´ (14 October 1976), p.532, para. B13.

57   House of Commons Official Report, Parliamentary Debates (_Hansard_), Session 1975-76, Fifth Series, Vol.917, 19 October 1976, _Written Answers_, col.369.

58   Lea and Young, _What is to be done about Law and Order?_, _supra_ note 27, pp.135-138.

59   Select Committee on Race Relations and Immigration, Session 1971-72, _Police/Immigrant Relations_, _supra_ note 35, Vol.1, _Report_, pp.22-25; Vol.2, _Evidence_, pp.89, 211, 220; Vol.3, _Evidence, Documents and Index_, p.670.

60   _Ibid._, Vol.1, _Report_, p.22, para. 66.

61   Indeed by 1976 the view of the Metropolitan Police was `in fact the involvement of black people in the arrest figures is disproportionate in respect of _every main category of crime´_ (emphasis added), Select Committee on Race Relations and Immigration, Session 1976-77, _The West Indian Community_, _supra_ note 30, Vol.2, _Evidence_, `Memorandum by the Metropolitan Police´, p.180, para.14. In view of the unreliability and vagaries of the crime statistics the assertion _in fact_ seemed rather inappropriate.

62   F.H. McClintock, _Crimes of Violence_, London: Macmillan, 1963, but see T. Morris, `Crimes of violence: review of McClintock´, _Institute of Race Relations Newsletter_, February 1964; see also A.E.

Bottoms, `Delinquency among immigrants: a further note´, Race, Vol.9, October 1967; A.E. Bottoms and P. Wiles, `Race, crime and violence´, in F.J. Ebling (ed.), Racial Variation in Man, London: Institute of Biology, 1975. For further discussion of crime in the period 1955-65 see F.H. McClintock and N.H. Avison, Crime in England and Wales, London: Heinemann, 1968 and criticisms of this study in L. McDonald, The Sociology of Law and Order, London: Faber, 1976.

63   John R. Lambert, Crime, Police and Race Relations, London: Oxford University Press, 1970, pp.124-5, and 281-91.

64   Maureen Cain, Society and the Policeman´s Role, London: Routledge and Kegan Paul, 1973, p.117.

65   Joseph A. Hunte, Nigger-Hunting in England?, London: West Indian Standing Conference, 1966.

66   Lea and Young, What is to be done about Law and Order?, supra note 27, p.138.

67   See Select Committee on Race Relations and Immigration, Session 1976-77, The West Indian Community, supra note 30, Vol.3, Evidence and Appendices, `Additional Memorandum by the Metropolitan Police´ (December 1976), Annex A, p.701, paras. 13-14.

68   The relationship between unemployment and crime is a complicated one as pointed out by Kenneth Roberts, `Youth unemployment and urban unrest´ in John Benyon (ed.), Scarman and After, Oxford: Pergamon Press,

1984, pp.181-83; see also, T. Crick, `Black youth, crime and related problems´, <u>Youth in Society</u>, Vol.40, 1980, pp.20-22.

69   These quotations, and the basic argument, are from Jim Bulpitt, <u>Continuity, Autonomy and Peripheralisation: The Anatomy of the Centre´s Race Statecraft in England</u>, paper presented to the seminar on `Race and Politics´ at Oxford, 28-30 September 1984, pp.8-11 and 32-33; this is published as chapter one in Z. Layton-Henry and P. Rich (eds), <u>Race, Government and Politics in Britain</u>, London : Macmillan, 1986; for further discussion of analysis of Centre-Periphery relations see Jim Bulpitt, <u>Territory and Power in the United Kingdom: An Interpretation</u>, Manchester: Manchester University Press, 1983.

70   Select Committee on Race Relations and Immigration, Session 1971-72, <u>Police/Immigrant Relations</u>, <u>supra</u> note 35, <u>Report</u>, p.92, para 342.

71   Bulpitt, <u>Continuity, Autonomy and Peripheralisation</u>, <u>supra</u> note 69, p.32.

72   Greaves, `The Brixton disorders´, <u>supra</u> note 15; Demuth, `<u>Sus´: a Report on the Vagrancy Act</u>, <u>supra</u> note 16; Stevens and Willis, <u>Race, Crime and Arrests</u>, <u>supra</u> note 17; House of Commons, <u>Race Relations and the `Sus´ Law</u>, <u>supra</u> note 18; Brogden, `"Sus" is dead but what about "Sas"?´, <u>supra</u> note 19; Willis, <u>The Use, Effectiveness and Impact of Police Stop and Search Powers</u>, <u>supra</u> note 20; <u>Police and People in London</u>, <u>supra</u> note 21; see also S. Pulle, <u>Police-Immigrant Relations in Ealing</u>, London: Runnymede Trust, 1973.

73   The Brixton Disorders, supra note 3, paras.
      4.11-4.20.

74   H. Mannheim, Comparative Criminology, London:
      Routledge and Kegan Paul, 1965, Vol.1, p.114.

75   Louis Blom-Cooper and Richard Drabble, `Police
      perception of crime: Brixton and the operational
      response´, British Journal of Criminology, Vol.22,
      April 1982, pp.184-87.

76   Police and People in London, Vol.4: David J. Smith
      and Jeremy Gray, The Police in Action, London:
      Policy Studies Institute, 1983 (PSI No.621), p.128.

77   The Brixton Disorders, supra note 3, para. 4.22.

78   Daily Mail, 21 January 1982.

79   For each reported offence the Metropolitan Police
      record the extent of any injuries. It appears that
      injuries ranging from slight to fatal occur in about
      half of all robbery cases and in less than one out
      of ten `other violent thefts´, that is 90 per cent
      of `other violent thefts´ involve no injury at all:
      Stevens and Willis, Race, Crime and Arrests, supra
      note 17, pp.36-37. This study also examined the
      degree of injury caused, by the ethnic group of the
      assailant, and found that contrary to popular
      perceptions attacks by black people are much less
      likely to result in any injuries; the analysis is
      for all crimes of violence, that is assaults,
      robberies and `other violent thefts.´

Attacker's Identification

Degree of Injury	White	`Coloured`	Mixed	Not known	Total
	(n=19114)	(n=7164)	(n=4553)	(n=870)	(n=6527)
Fatal	2.8	0.8	0.2	0.4	1.4
Serious	8.8	5.5	8.6	5.8	7.0
Slight	66.7	49.4	53.2	63.8	61.0
None	21.8	44.2	37.9	30.0	30.7
Total	100.1	99.9	99.9	100.0	100.1

Attackers in reported crimes of violence by injury caused (Metropolitan Police District 1975 in percentages).
Source: Stevens and Willis, Race, Crime and Arrests, supra note 17, p.37.

80   For further discussion of the press coverage see Graham Murdock, `Reporting the riots: images and impact` in John Benyon (ed.), Scarman and After, Oxford: Pergamon Press, 1984, pp.90-93; see also The Runnymede Trust, Bulletin, `Race and Immigration` No.143, 1982.

81   J. Shirley, `Mugging: statistics of an "unacceptable crime"`, The Guardian, 14 March 1982.

82   `Black, white and full statistics`, The Guardian 24 March 1983.

83   The Brixton Disorders, supra note 3, paras. 4.1-4.2
      and 4.43.

84   Working Party into Community/Police Relations in
      Lambeth, Final Report London: Borough of Lambeth,
      January 1981.

85   Francis Wheen, `Living in a state of siege', New
      Statesman, Vol.101, No.2602, 30 January 1981, p.10.

86   The Brixton Disorders, supra note 3, para. 4.33.

87   Greaves, `The Brixton disorders', supra note 15,
      p.64.

88   The Standard, 23 April 1982; The Times, 24 April
      1982, `Law Report'; The Daily Telegraph, 24 April
      1982; The Guardian, 24 April 1982.

89   Institute of Race Relations, Police Against Black
      People, London: Institute of Race Relations, 1979;
      Derek Humphry, Police Power and Black People,
      London: Panther, 1972; Paul Gordon, White Law, supra
      note 14.

90   Select Committee on Race Relations and Immigration,
      Session 1971-72, Police/Immigrant Relations, supra
      note 35, Vol.2, Evidence, p.72, para. 221.

91   Select Committee on Race Relations and Immigration,
      Session 1976-77, The West Indian Community, supra
      note 30, Vol.3, Evidence and Appendices, pp.432-433,
      para. 1103

92   Rights, Vol.7, No.1, Spring 1983, p.6.

93   Select Committee on Race Relations and Immigration, Session 1971-72, Police/Immigrant Relations, supra note 35, Vol.2, Evidence, `Memorandum by "B" Division of the Metropolitan Police´, pp.213-214; `Memorandum by London Council of Social Services Committee for Inter-Racial Co-operation´, pp.231-232 and 265-267; Vol.3, Evidence, Documents and Index, `Memorandum by the National Council for Civil Liberties´, p.623, `Memorandum from the Institute of Race Relations´, p.770; See also Gordon, White Law, supra note 14, pp.39-40.

94   House of Commons Official Report, Parliamentary Debates (Hansard), Session 1980-81, Sixth Series, Vol.8, 16 July 1981, col. 1425.

95   House of Commons Official Report, Parliamentary Debates (Hansard), Session 1980-81, Sixth Series, Vol.10, 29 October 1981, cols. 991-998; House of Commons Official Report, Parliamentary Debates (Hansard), Session 1982-83, Sixth Series, Vol.41, 28 April 1983, col.372; Policing London, No.8, June/July 1983, pp.6-7; New Law Journal, Vol.133, No.6100, 22 April 1983, p.363; Report of the Police Complaints Board 1982, HC 278, London: HMSO, 12 April 1983, p.1.

96   Peter Southgate and Paul Ekblom, Contacts between Police and Public: Findings from the British Crime Survey, London: HMSO, 1984 (Home Office Research Study No.77), pp.23-24.

97   Report of the Police Complaints Board 1983, HC 391, London: HMSO, 25 April 1984, pp.5-8 and 16-22.

98   Philip Stevens and Carole Willis, <u>Ethnic Minorities</u>
        <u>and Complaints Against the Police</u>, London: Home
        Office, 1981 (Research and Planning Unit Paper 5);
        see also Robert Moore, <u>Racism and Black Resistance</u>,
        London: Pluto, 1975; Anthony Judge, `The police and
        the coloured communities: a police view´, <u>New</u>
        <u>Community</u>, Vol.3, No.3, Summer 1974; Stephen Box,
        <u>Power, Crime and Mystification</u>, London: Tavistock,
        1983, pp.82-91.

99   For example P. Evans, <u>Attitudes of Young Immigrants</u>,
        London: Runnymede Trust 1972; in another survey of
        black and white people under 25 nearly 80 per cent
        of the blacks agreed with the statement `around
        here, the police often pick on black people´:
        Community Relations Commission, <u>Unemployment and</u>
        <u>Homelessness: A Report</u>, London: HMSO, 1974.

100   See Simon Field, <u>The Attitudes of Ethnic Minorities</u>,
        London: HMSO, 1984 (Home Office Research Study
        No.80), ch.7 `Attitudes towards the police´; see
        also literature cited earlier <u>supra</u> notes 14 and 19.

101   <u>Police and People in London</u>, Vol.1: Smith, <u>A Survey</u>
        <u>of Londoners</u>, <u>supra</u> note 21, p.325 and ch.9, `Views
        about standards of police conduct´, pp.236-273.

102   Peter Fryer, <u>Staying Power: The History of Black</u>
        <u>People in Britain</u>, London: Pluto Press, 1984,
        pp.395-96; Bethnal Green and Stepney Trades Council,
        <u>Blood on the Streets: A Report on Racial Attacks in</u>
        <u>East London</u>, London: the Trades Council, 1978; see
        also Commission for Racial Equality, <u>Brick Lane and</u>
        <u>Beyond: An Inquiry into Racial Strife and Violence</u>
        <u>in Tower Hamlets</u>, London: CRE, 1979.

103   Tony Jefferson and Roger Grimshaw, Controlling the
        Constable: Police Accountability in England and
        Wales, London: Muller, 1984, pp.104-135; Gordon,
        White Law, supra note 14, pp.29-30; Unofficial
        Committee of Inquiry, Report: Southall 23 April
        1979, London: NCCL, 1980; Unofficial Committee of
        Inquiry, The Death of Blair Peach, London: NCCL,
        1981; State Research, State Research Bulletin,
        June-July 1979.

104   Jefferson and Grimshaw, Controlling the Constable,
        supra note 103, p.105.

105   The Daily Telegraph, 24 April 1979, quoted in
        Unofficial Committee of Inquiry, Report: Southall 23
        April 1979, supra note 103, pp.159-160.

106   Southall Rights, 23 April 1979: A Report, Southall:
        Southall Rights, 1980.

107   Home Office, Racial Attacks: Report of a Home Office
        Study, London: HMSO, November 1981; Francesca Klug,
        Racist Attacks, London: Runnymede Trust, 1982;
        Greater London Council Police Committee, Racial
        Harassment in London, London: Greater London
        Council, 1984; see also, Joint Committee Against
        Racialism, Racial Violence in Britain, London: JCAR,
        1981; Searchlight June 1982 and August 1982; Ealing
        Community Relations Council, Racialist Activity in
        Ealing 1979-81, London Ealing CRC, 1981; Commission
        for Racial Equality, Racial Harassment on Local
        Authority Housing Estates: A Report prepared by the
        London Race and Housing Forum, London: CRE, 1981.

108   Greater London Council, Racial Harassment in London,
        supra note 107, p.18.

109   <u>Police and People in London</u>, Vol.4: Smith and Gray,
       <u>The Police in Action</u>, <u>supra</u> note 76, pp.155-162.

110   <u>The Guardian</u>, 8 December 1983 and 9 December 1983;
       <u>Policing London</u>, No.11, February/March 1984,
       pp.54-55; see also Paul Harrison, <u>Inside the Inner
       City</u>, Harmondsworth: Penguin, 1983, ch.18 `The
       roughest beat´ and ch. 19 `Brother shall strike
       brother´, pp.347-397; see further David Clark,
       `Racial assaults way of life in East End´, <u>The
       Observer</u>, 4 March 1984, p.20 where it is said that
       bricks through windows, verbal abuse, petrol
       bombings, casual street violence and a `totally
       inadequate police response´ are now the way of life:
       `It´s just that Asian people have got used to being
       spat at, sworn at, having bottles thrown at them or
       having their windows broken. The police tend to
       treat these things as neighbourhood disputes, when
       they clearly aren´t´. Ian Mikardo, M.P., said `I´m
       sorry to say that the police are not as active if
       it´s an assault on a black person as they are if the
       victim is white´.

111   Reported in <u>Policing London</u>, Vol.3, No.16,
       January/March 1985, pp.22-23.

112   See for example the <u>TV Eye</u> programme (Thames
       Television) entitled `Racial Outlaws´ broadcast on
       17 January 1985; `East End Asians bear the brunt of
       growth in racist attacks´, <u>The Guardian</u>, 17 January
       1985; `Reporting racial harassment´, <u>The Guardian</u>,
       28 January 1985; `Policing the race hate gangs´, <u>The
       Times</u>, 8 February 1985 and 9 February 1985.

113   Greater London Council, <u>Racial Harassment in London</u>,
       <u>supra</u> note 107, p.12.

114   Paul Gordon, <u>Passport Raids and Checks</u>, London: Runnymede Trust, 1981; Gordon, <u>White Law</u>, <u>supra</u> note 14, pp.35-42; see also Paul Gordon, <u>Deportations and Removals</u>, London: Runnymede Trust, 1984; Manchester Law Centre, <u>The Thin End of the White Wedge</u>, Manchester: Law Centre, 1981; Institute of Race Relations, <u>Police Against Black People</u>, <u>supra</u> note 14.

115   Colin Brown, <u>Black and White Britain: The Third PSI Survey</u>, London: Heinemann, 1984, table 138, p.276; see also tables 57 and 119, pp.122 and 221.

116   <u>Ibid</u>., pp.256-263.

117   <u>Police and People in London</u>, Vol.4: Smith and Gray, <u>The Police in Action</u>, <u>supra</u> note 76, p.332.

118   <u>The Brixton Disorders</u>, <u>supra</u> note 3, para. 4.22.

119   Humphry, <u>Police Power and Black People</u>, <u>supra</u> note 89, p.11.

120   Royal Commission on Criminal Procedure (Chairman: Sir Cyril Philips), <u>Report</u>, London: HMSO, January 1981 (Cmnd. 8092); see also Royal Commission on Criminal Procedure, <u>The Investigation and Prosecution of Criminal Offences in England and Wales: The Law and Procedure</u>, London: HMSO, 1981 (Cmnd. 8092-1).

121   For a discussion of the Police and Criminal Evidence Act in particular, and policing problems in general, see John Benyon and Colin Bourn (eds.), <u>The Police: Powers, Procedures and Proprieties</u>, Oxford: Pergamon Press, 1986; see also articles in <u>Police</u> and <u>Police Review</u>, various issues 1985.

122   Robert Reiner, <u>The Blue-Coated Worker</u>, Cambridge:
       Cambridge University Press, 1978, pp.225-226; see
       also R. Reiner, `Black and blue: race and the
       police´ <u>New Society</u>, 17 September 1981; R. Reiner,
       `Who are the police?´ <u>The Political Quarterly</u>,
       Vol.53, No.2, April-June 1982; R. Reiner, `The
       police and race relations´, in J. Baxter and L.
       Koffman (eds.), <u>Police: The Constitution and the
       Community</u>, London: Professional Books, 1985.

123   Peter Southgate, <u>Police Probationer Training in Race
       Relations</u>, London: Home Office, 1982 (Research and
       Planning Unit Paper No.8), pp.9-12; see also Simon
       Holdaway, <u>Inside the British Police</u>, Oxford:
       Blackwell, 1983, pp.66-71.

124   See `The enormous price of "a slip of the tongue"´,
       <u>Police</u>, Vol.16, June 1984, p.3.

125   <u>Police and People in London</u>, Vol.4. Smith and Gray,
       <u>The Police in Action</u>, <u>supra</u> note 76, pp.109 and 127.

126   <u>Coventry Evening Telegraph</u>, 26 November 1981; <u>The
       Brixton Disorders</u>, <u>supra</u> note 3, para.5.15.

127   Police Training Council, <u>Community and Race
       Relations Training for the Police</u>, London: Home
       Office, 1983; C. Bainbridge,`Pilot study of racism
       awareness training´, <u>Police Journal</u>, Vol.57, No.2,
       1984, pp.165-169; Peter Southgate, <u>Racism Awareness
       Training for the Police</u>, London: Home Office, 1984
       (Research and Planning Unit Paper No.29); Michael
       Banton, `Back to the drawing board´, <u>Police</u>, Vol.17,
       February 1985, pp.34 and 44; Maureen Baker, `Come
       down to earth, Professor!´, <u>Police</u>, Vol.17, April
       1985, p.48.

128   A. Colman and L. Gorman, `Conservatism, dogmatism
        and authoritarianism in British police officers´,
        Sociology, February 1982; A.J.P. Butler letter in
        The Times, 5 October 1981; P.A.J. Waddington,
        `Conservatism, dogmatism and authoritarianism in the
        police: a comment´, Sociology, November 1982; A.
        Colman, `Rejoinder´, Sociology, August 1983; `Police
        racism in the making´, Policing London, No.4,
        November 1982, pp.1-2; P.Taylor, `How Hendon police
        cadets are wooed away from racialism´, Police,
        Vol.15, August 1983.

129   Police and People in London, Vol.4: Smith and Gray,
        The Police in Action, supra note 76, pp.150-154;
        David Wilson, Simon Holdaway and Christopher
        Spencer, `Black police in the United Kingdom´,
        Policing, Vol.1, No.1, Autumn 1984, pp.20-30.

130   Mike Hough and Pat Mayhew, The British Crime Survey:
        first report, London: HMSO, 1983 (Home Office
        Research Study No.76); Southgate and Ekblom,
        Contacts between Police and Public, supra note 96;
        David Moxon and Peter Jones `Public reactions to
        police behaviour: some findings from the British
        Crime Survey´, Policing, Vol.1, No.1, Autumn 1984,
        pp.49-56.

131   Police and People in London, Vol.1: Smith, A survey
        of Londoners supra note 21, pp.181-185 and 219-224.

132   Hough and Mayhew, The British Crime Survey, supra
        note 130, p.29; see also Southgate and Ekblom,
        Contacts between Police and Public supra note 96.

133   Southgate, Police Probationer Training in Race
        Relations supra note 123, pp.4-15.

134   The Brixton Disorders, _supra_ note 3, paras.
        5.33-5.40.

135   Robert Reiner, The Politics of the Police, Brighton:
        Wheatsheaf, 1985, pp.126-127 and 134; see also _supra_
        note 122.

136   See G. Greaves, `The Brixton disorders´ in John
        Benyon (ed.), Scarman and After, Oxford: Pergamon
        Press, 1984; pp.69-71; for a discussion of the
        concept see David Mason, `After Scarman: a note on
        the concept of "institutional racism"´ New
        Community, Vol.10, Summer 1982, pp.38-45; see also
        Michael Banton, `The concept of racism´ and John Rex
        `The concept of race in sociological theory´ in S.
        Zubaida, Race and Racialism, London: Tavistock,
        1970.

137   Gordon, White Law, _supra_ note 14, p.137; see also
        Robert Miles and Annie Phizacklea, White Man´s
        Country: Racism in British Politics, London: Pluto,
        1984; A. Sivanandan, A Different Hunger, London:
        Pluto, 1982; Martin Barker, The New Racism, London:
        Junction, 1981; Hall et al., Policing the Crisis,
        supra note 43, especially part 3, pp.181-397; Fryer,
        Staying Power, _supra_ note 102.

138   Salman Rushdie, `The new empire within Britain´, New
        Society, 9 December 1982.

139   John Rex, `Law and order in multi-racial inner city
        areas - the issues after Scarman´ in Philip Norton
        (ed.), Law and Order and British Politics,
        Aldershot: Gower, 1984, p.107.

140   The Brixton Disorders, _supra_ note 3, paras.2.22 and
        4.62.

141   Reiner, <u>The Politics of the Police</u>, <u>supra</u> note 135, pp.134-135 and 204-205.

142   Simha Landau, `Juveniles and the police´, <u>British Journal of Criminology</u>, Vol.21, January 1981.

143   The most important recent book is Reiner´s, <u>The Politics of the Police</u>, <u>supra</u> note 135; see also Robert Baldwin and Richard Kinsey, <u>Police Powers and Politics</u>, London: Quartet, 1982; Jefferson and Grimshaw, <u>Controlling the Constable</u>, <u>supra</u> note 103; Tony Bunyan, <u>The History and Practice of the Political Police in Britain</u>, London: Quartet, 1977; Michael Brogden, <u>The Police: Autonomy and Consent</u>, London: Academic, 1982; D. Pope and N. Weiner (eds.), <u>Modern Policing</u>, London: Croom Helm, 1981.

144   Robert Reiner, `Is Britain turning into a police state?´, <u>New Society</u>, 2 August 1984, pp 51-56; see also Robert Reiner, `A watershed in policing´, <u>The Political Quarterly</u>, Vol.56, April-June 1985, pp.122-131

145   See for example Robert Mark, <u>Policing a Perplexed Society</u>, London: Allen and Unwin, 1977 and R. Mark, <u>In the Office of Constable</u>, London: Collins, 1978.

146   <u>The Guardian</u>, 17 March 1982.

147   `Anderton attacks political policing´, <u>The Guardian</u>, 8 June 1985.

148   The `<u>Brixton Disorders</u>, <u>supra</u> note 3, paras. 5.3 and 5.58.

149   Basil Griffiths, `One-tier policing´, in John Benyon
       (ed.), Scarman and After, Oxford: Pergamon Press,
       1984, p.128.

150   Harrison, Inside the Inner City, supra note 110,
       p.362.

151   P.A.J. Waddington, `"Community policing": a
       sceptical appraisal´, in Norton (ed.), Law and Order
       and British Politics, supra, note 139, p. 95.

152   For further discussion see John Benyon, Legitimacy,
       Conflict, Order: Urban Disadvantage and Political
       Stability in Britain, paper presented at the
       European Consortium for Political Research joint
       workshops in Barcelona, 25-30 March 1985.

153   T. Gurr, Why Men Rebel, Princeton : Princeton
       University Press, 1970; T. Gurr, `A causal model of
       civil strife´, American Political Science Review,
       Vol. 62, 1968, pp. 1104-1124; C. Johnson,
       Revolutionary Change, London : University of London
       Press, 1968

APPENDIX A

A chronicle of civil commotion in 1985

Summer 1985   Reports of clashes between youths and police in Birmingham, London, Liverpool and elsewhere; armed raids by police in Brixton and West Midlands; increase in tension reported in areas such as Handsworth and Tottenham, as police seek to clamp down on minor offences.

24 August   John Shorthouse, aged 5, shot dead during an armed raid in Birmingham; later uniformed police are attacked and a WPC is badly beaten.

30 August   Toxteth police station attacked by demonstrators, protesting at the arrest of four black youths; in Brixton it is alleged that armed police searching for drugs break down the front door of Paula Belsham's house, and hold a gun to her head, and subject her to an intimate examination [reported in the press, and in the House of Commons, 23 October].

1 September   A new organisation called Anti-Fascist Action is formed, to resist by force the growing wave of racist attacks.

2 September   In the Cabinet reshuffle, Douglas Hurd replaces Leon Brittan as Home Secretary, and Kenneth Baker steps into Patrick Jenkin's place at the Department of the Environment.

3 September   Kenneth Oxford, Chief Constable of Merseyside, threatens to end community foot patrol policing in Liverpool 8 (Toxteth) if the attacks on officers persist.

5 September   Liverpool City Council announces that its 31,000 employees are to receive redundancy notices, as its funds will run out by Christmas.

7-8 September   Handsworth Festival takes place: little trouble reported as carnival revellers and local police dance in the streets.

9 September*	At about 11.30 on this Monday morning an Asian shopkeeper is stabbed in the arm outside the bank in Villa Road. In the late afternoon, a police
5.15-5.45pm	officer issues a parking ticket to a black driver; there are allegations of racial abuse; further police arrive, and there are accusations that a young woman is pushed by an officer; during the ensuing fight between bystanders and the police, 11 officers are reported injured and a number of police vehicles damaged.
7.40pm	Villa Cross Hall is reported to be on fire, and fire officers who arrive are warned by youths not to tackle the blaze.
7.55pm	Police officers who try to help the fire brigade are attacked by youths throwing bricks and petrol bombs.
8.15pm	Some other buildings are burning, and shops being looted. More police arrive and chase youths in vicinity of Villa Cross pub.
9.00pm	Several premises in Lozells Road, including garage, are blazing; rioters control area: sealed off by burning cars.
9.00-11.30pm	Further looting and attacks on the police; 45 properties on fire, including the post office; 650 police officers appear unable to regain control.
11.30pm	Police gradually succeed in fighting their way into the area, negotiating burning barricades in Lozells Road and other streets; water from firehoses short circuits electricity.
midnight	Although the police still sustain some attacks, the rioting winds down, and fire officers deluge buildings with water.
10 September*	
3.00am	Still chaotic with fires burning, as looters return to retrieve goods hidden in gardens.
4.00am	Order is restored.
7.00am	The bodies of Amirali and Kassamali Moledina are discovered in the smouldering wreckage of the post office; (a 21-year-old white man was subsequently charged with their murder).
morning	Groups of bewildered people congregate, surveying the devastation, surrounded by cohorts of reporters.
1.30pm	The Home Secretary arrives in a convoy of cars; as he tries to talk to people shouts of abuse are followed by bricks, and he is forced to make a speedy exit in a police van.
2.10pm	Further burning, stoning and looting occurs; vehicles, including a police van and ITN car, are overturned and set on fire.
3.00pm	Sporadic incidents continue for some hours, and despite a heavy police presence there are accounts of people being robbed in shops by gangs, and of general lawlessness.
evening	Over 1400 police officers flood the area; some attacks are made on them, but their policy of

keeping crowds moving succeeds in avoiding further serious disorder.
The police report that the 291 arrested people are drawn from every racial and religious group, and the vast majority live in Handsworth;   11 casualties are reported, including 2 dead, 74 police injured, 35 members of the public injured; 83 premises and 23 vehicles have been damaged.

Outbreaks of disorder are reported elsewhere in the West Midlands, such as those in Dudley, West Bromwich and Moseley.

11 September   Mrs Thatcher describes those who complain about unemployment as `moaning minnies´;   at Birmingham Law Courts, where 75 people are facing charges arising out of the disturbances, there are demonstrations and fights break out;   at the SDP conference in Torquay, Dr Owen says that `none of us´ have taken Lord Scarman´s report seriously enough;   disorders are reported in Coventry and Wolverhampton.

12 September   Cabinet decides that there should be no judicial public inquiry into the disorder;   Home Secretary says the riots were `not a cry for help, but a cry for loot´;   Shadow Home Secretary asks why they occurred in an inner city area with high unemployment, and not in the Home Secretary´s constituency of Witney, where unemployment is low. Two white teenagers are sentenced to 3 years in custody for abusing and firebombing an Asian family in Stockwell Park Estate, London.

13 September   A series of crimes occur in St Paul´s district of Bristol, which was the scene of serious disorder in April 1980;   unrest is reported in the area; at the ACPO conference in Preston, the chief constables tell the Home Secretary of the need for an increase in police numbers.

14 September   The Asian members of Birmingham Community Relations Council resign, protesting that there has been insufficient condemnation of the violence in Handsworth.

16 September   Ex-Labour MP Julius Silverman is chosen to chair the inquiry by Birmingham City Council into the disturbances.

20 September   Mr Enoch Powell makes a widely-condemned speech which seems to call for a policy of repatriation.

28 September*   At 7 o´clock on this Saturday morning a posse of police, some armed and others with dogs, raid a house in Normandy Road, Brixton.   It is later reported to be the fifty-first armed raid in

7.00am   Brixton in 1985.   After the front door is broken

	down, two shots are fired by the police, who are searching for Mr Michael Groce, a man wanted for questioning for possession of a shotgun. His mother, a 38-year-old black woman, Mrs Cherry Groce, is hit by a bullet which causes her extremely serious injury.
morning	Rumours spread throughout Brixton that Mrs Groce is dead; tension grows as crowd gathers outside her house.
2.00pm	Bottle thrown at police superintendent in car; deputation goes to police station to protest about shooting; crowd gathers outside.
3.15pm	Youths rampage down Normandy Road, attacking reporters and camera crew.
5.15pm	A group marches in protest to Brixton Police Station, on the corner of Gresham Road and Brixton Road.
5.50pm	About 300 youths attack police station with bricks and petrol bombs; station is under siege until riot police disperse crowd at about 6.15pm.
6.35pm	In Brixton Road, motorists are stopped and their cars are set alight; some looting occurs.
7.15pm	The police are unable to contain disorder, and the rioting spreads.
8.30pm	Extensive looting takes place; a number of robberies occur; running battles in various streets; more cars set on fire.
9.30pm	The police advance from Coldharbour Lane into Brixton Road, beating riot shields; a large crowd of spectators contains some people who taunt the police, who now appear to be on the defensive.
11.00pm	Still extensive disorder; some buildings on fire.
midnight	Police tactics suddenly change, and without warning officers charge into spectators, hitting out with their truncheons; a number of people are hurt and/or arrested.

29 September*

2.30am	Rioting has ended.
afternoon	Crowds of youths gather and are moved on; serious allegations are later made that some police officers attacked residences on the Angell Estate; others allege abuse and assault; police report prolonged provocation.
6.30pm	Sporadic clashes occur between youths and police, and these continue into the night. The Metropolitan Police report that 43 members of the public and 10 police officers had been injured; 55 vehicles and a number of properties had been burned. Nearly a half of the 230 people arrested were white; a staggering 724 serious crimes were recorded, including 2 rapes, a number of assaults and robberies, and over 90 burglaries. During the disorder a freelance photographer, Mr David Hodge, sustained injuries from which he died three weeks later.

30 September Commander Alex Marnoch says police are investigating the role of political extremists in

the disorder; at the Labour Party conference the
behaviour of some police officers is bitterly
criticised.

1 October*   Officers from the District Support Unit mount a
               stop and search operation, in a search for drugs,
               on all cars entering the Broadwater Farm Estate in
               Tottenham. In Liverpool, 4 black men are remanded
               in custody on charges arising from disturbances on
               10 August; scuffles occur between people
               supporting them and police officers.
afternoon   tension grows in Liverpool 8 (Toxteth); crowds
               gather and barricades are erected.
5pm   Officers from the Operational Support Division
               (OSD) seek to disperse youths by driving police
               landrovers, on the pavements as well as in the
               road, into the crowds.
5.30pm   Two motorists are pulled from their cars, which
               are set on fire in Upper Parliament Street; other
               vehicles are set alight, and a TV crew is forced
               to hand over a £20,000 camera.
7.15pm   The disorder appears to have died down.
7.55pm   Rioting begins again, with the violence primarily
               directed against the police; Archbishop Derek
               Worlock says the behaviour earlier of the OSD
               caused great anger; the disturbances continue
               until after midnight; police report 14 public and
               4 police injuries, 13 arrests and a number of
               properties and vehicles damaged by fire.

               Disorder also occurs in Peckham, in south London;
               some shops are damaged, and clashes take place
               between youths and the police; a large area is
               effectively sealed off from 10pm until 2.30am, and
               some people trying to re-enter Peckham to return
               to their homes complain that police turned them
               away, and were abusive to black people. In north
               London, police are put on the alert for riots at
               Broadwater Farm, after a series of hoax phone
               calls which, it is believed, are intended to lure
               police into a trap.

2 October   Criminal Statistics [Cmnd 9621] reveals that
               during 1984 in England and Wales the police
               recorded nearly 3.5 million notifiable crimes, an
               increase of 8 per cent on the preceding year.

3 October   The Home Secretary reports to the Cabinet on the
               riots, but a public inquiry is firmly ruled out.
               The unemployment figures for September are
               announced, and these reveal that 3,346,198 are
               registered as jobless (13.8%); this is the
               highest total ever recorded.

4 October   Douglas Hurd tours Brixton; the funeral of
               John Shorthouse (5) who was shot on 24 August,
               takes place.

5 October*	Nine Anglican clergymen in Brixton issue a statement which strongly deplores the behaviour of some police in the area, the actions of the rioters, and social and economic conditions.
1.00pm	Police stop Floyd Jarrett, a 23-years-old black man, as the tax disc on his BMW car is out of date. Jarrett, who is well known in the area as a worker at the Broadwater Farm Youth Association, explains that he has not had a chance to renew the tax as he has only just returned from a youth exchange trip to Jamaica. The officers search his car for stolen goods, finding none, and Jarrett protests about the delay and its effect on his pregnant girl friend who is in the car. A row develops which results in Jarrett being arrested for assaulting an officer, although both he and his girl friends deny that such an assault occurred. Jarrett is later acquitted of the charge of assault. He is taken to Tottenham Police Station.
afternoon	The arrested man claims that he is assaulted, detained for five hours without being allowed to make a phone call, and then released with his possessions returned, minus the front door key to his mother's house. The police claim that he is treated correctly.
5.00pm	Five police officers enter the home of Mrs Cynthia Jarrett, in Thorpe Street, Tottenham, about a mile from Broadwater Farm Estate. The police claim that the front door was open, the Jarrett family claim that officers used the key taken from Floyd. Police search the house for stolen goods, of which none are found, and during this period Mrs Jarrett (49) collapses and dies. The family allege assault, the police deny this strongly.
evening	News of Mrs Jarrett's death spreads round the area.
6 October* 12.00 noon	As rumours abound about police involvement in the death, a meeting is held at Tottenham Police Station between officers and community leaders, including Floyd Jarrett.
2.00pm	A crowd of about 50 gathers outside the station; abuse is exchanged with officers, and there is damage to vehicles.
3.30pm	The windscreen of a police car, called to Broadwater Farm Estate by a hoax call, is shattered; one officer is injured in the eye by glass and is taken to hospital. Sporadic violence occurs.
6.00pm	A meeting is held at the Broadwater Farm Community Centre, to which the police are not invited; Dolly Kiffin and Councillor Bernie Grant appeal for calm, but are told to leave.
6.50pm	In answer to a hoax phone call, a police transit van arrives and is attacked in Willan Road.

7.05pm	Police District Support Units (DSUs) are attacked; trouble erupts in The Avenue.
7.45pm	Crowd of youths run down The Avenue towards police, overturning vehicles and setting fire to them; cars are driven at police lines.
8.55pm	A major fire is burning, and police try to advance.
9.30pm	Supermarket in Willan Road on fire; police beaten back by missiles and attacks from riots.
9.44pm	Man with sawn-off shotgun fires at police in Griffin Road, injuring two journalists and a sound man.
9.45pm	Policeman is seriously injured by bullet from a gun.
9.49pm	A police constable is hit in the leg by the blast from a shotgun, which causes bad injuries.
10.10pm	Flats in Moira Close are on fire; 7 firemen and 10 police who go to tackle the blaze are attacked by a gang of youths.
10.15pm	While retreating from the attack, PC Keith Blakelock slips and is fatally stabbed by several assailants.
10.17pm	PC Blakelock is dragged clear by fire officer.
10.20pm	Gas explosion in Adams Road.
10.30pm	A gun is fired in Griffin Road, and the bullet grazes a police officer's head.
11.00pm	Keith Blakelock is certified dead at North Middlesex Hospital; D11 squad arrive at Broadwater Farm Estate with CS Gas and plastic bullets; other officers cheer their arrival, but they are not used.
11.20pm	Helicopter hovers above the riot, picking out participants in powerful searchlight.
12.05pm	Disorder peters out as rioters drift away.
7 October*	Commissioner of Police for the Metropolis, Sir Kenneth Newman, inspects scene and
1.10am	assesses the position.
4.00am	Police move cautiously into the estate.
morning	Local residents and hordes of reporters survey the wreckage. Tension remains high, but large contingents of police prevent any recurrence of serious disorder.

Police report that casualties were: one police
officer killed, 223 police and 20 public injured,
and extensive damage to cars and premises by fire.
It is believed that three separate firearms were
used during the disorders. Subsequently, a number
of arrests are made, including 5 for the murder of
PC Blakelock. Police do not discover guns on the
estate.

Sir Kenneth Newman `puts all people of London on
notice' that he will not shrink from using plastic
bullets if necessary; the Home Secretary supports
use of CS gas or other implements to suppress
disorder.

10 October	After Leicester versus Derby football match, serious disorder occurs in Highfield district of the city; fighting and looting occurs; petrol bombs are thrown and several hundred police are needed to quell the youths. At the Conservative Party conference, Douglas Hurd calls council leaders such as Ted Knight (Lambeth) and Bernie Grant (Haringey) `the high priests of race conflict´ and he announces a new offence of disorderly conduct, which will be included in the Public Order Bill.
11 October	T&GWU and NUPE members of Haringey Council workforce call a 24-hour strike in protest at Mr Grant´s remarks that `the police got a bloody good hiding´ at Broadwater Farm; they demand that all forms of violence should be condemned; Grant´s supporters stage a counter demonstration. In her conference speech at Blackpool, Mrs Thatcher states that there can never be any justification for rioting, and she pledges that there will be more men and equipment for the police if necessary.
18 October	Funeral of Mrs Jarrett; ILEA NUT votes to refuse co-operation with the police, because of their alleged racist attitudes.
21 October	Home Secretary makes statement to the House of Commons.
23 October	Opposition motion for an independent judicial inquiry is defeated by 292 votes to 191.
Note: *	all times are approximate, as accounts vary; the times given are those upon which there is the most agreement
Sources	Newspaper and television reports; personal accounts; Scotland Yard releases and reports; Birmingham City Council inquiry hearings; Hansard, 21 October and 23 October 1985; interviews with local people.

APPENDIX B

Disorder in the devil's decade

A strange myth seems to have developed that despite high
unemployment, the 1930s was a period of relative public
tranquillity. Mrs Thatcher, for example, has remarked on a
number of occasions: 'we had much higher unemployment in the
1930s, but we didn't get violence then'. This view of the
inter war years reveals a dramatic case of historical
amnesia, for the period was far from peaceful. Indeed, as
noted by two historians who have made a special study of the
1930s, 'the Government was seriously alarmed by the threat to
public order' (Cook and Stevenson, 1979 : 218).

It might reasonably be asked of those who claim this was
a time when unemployment was high yet civil order was
assured, why did two successive governments feel it was
necessary for Parliament to pass public order legislation?
The Incitement to Disaffection Act 1934, and the Public Order
Act 1936, were considered essential to meet the perceived
challenge from extra-parliamentary movements. Public
disorder was seen as a threat not just by the governments in
the 1930s but also by the media. For example, The Times (29
October 1932) said of the National Unemployed Workers'
Movement (NUWM) Hunger March:

> The evil will grow if it is not checked. There are
> plenty of ways in which legitimate discontent may
> be rationally expressed. The government must
> seriously consider whether the spurious importance
> which these mass marches are bound to be given at
> home or abroad should not be countered by special
> restrictive measures.

Two years later, the Sunday Pictorial (22 February 1934) reported:

> BIG PLANS TO CURB `HUNGER MARCHERS´; Foiling a New Red Plot: It is known that sinister influences are at work to provoke trouble of a grave character and the authorities have not overlooked the possibility of repercussions in London following the desperate street fighting which recently took place in Paris and Vienna.

In the autumn of 1932, Sir Oswald Moseley formed the British Union of Fascists (BUF). In 1934, Lord Rothermere´s newspapers (the Daily Mail, the Evening News, the Sunday Dispatch and the Sunday Pictorial) started to support the fascists. On 15 January 1934, for example, the Daily Mail carried an article entitled `Hurrah for the Black-Shirts´. But BUF meetings were often accompanied by violent clashes, and its anti-semitism led to many attacks by fascists on Jewish people. On 4 October 1936 a march led by Mosley was confronted by a huge crowd of opponents, and the `Battle of Cable Street´ ensued, in London´s East End. The BUF continued in existence until May 1940 when Mosley and some of his followers were detained under the Emergency Powers Defence Regulations.

As the following selection of incidents shows, with good reason the 1930s earned its tag of the `devil´s decade´.

1930

Jan: NUWM reports membership still rising; its slogan is `on the streets with mass demonstrations´.
Mar: 3rd National Hunger March sets out.
Apr: race riots in North Shields.
May: struggle between hunger marchers and police at House of Commons.
Jul: riots between Roman Catholics and Orangemen in Everton, Liverpool.
Aug: baton charge on strikers in Cardiff.
Nov: affray at political meeting in Derby.

1931

Jan: at Highbury, crowds sweep police aside.
Mar: crime wave reported.
Jun: gang disorder in London.

Jul: Orange riots in Liverpool (50 hurt).
Aug: street battle in Oxford;   riot in Manchester: 1000
      fight police.
Sep: clashes between police and Welsh hunger marchers at
      Trades Union Congress in Bristol;   police baton
      unemployed marchers in Whitehall;   violence between
      unemployed and police in Dundee, Birmingham, Glasgow,
      and Manchester;   Royal Navy mutiny at Invergordon;
      trouble in Liverpool.
Oct: mounted police charge unemployed in Salford;   more
      rioting in Glasgow;   80,000 unemployed march in
      Manchester: police turn fire hoses on them;   many
      people clubbed by police;   violent clashes between
      police and unemployed in London, Blackburn and Cardiff;
      riot at Mosley meeting in Birmingham;   trouble at
      Leicester meeting;   more disturbances in London and
      Cardiff;   National Government under MacDonald elected.
Nov: disorder in Shoreditch, elsewhere in London and in
      Coventry;   marches and demonstrations against the means
      test.
Dec: police and unemployed clash in Liverpool, Wallsend,
      London, Leeds, Glasgow, Wigan, Kirkcaldy,
      Stoke-on-Trent and elsewhere.

                              1932

Jan: unemployed protest in Leicester;   clashes between
      police and jobless in Keighley, Glasgow, Rochdale, and
      Glasgow again.
Feb: violence in London and Bristol.
Mar: more clashes in Glasgow.
Apr: riots in London;   crowd rescue arrested men in Leeds;
      strike and protests in Hinckley;   growing crime wave is
      a source of concern.
Jun: police break up Communist march in Hendon;   mounted
      police charge march in Bristol;   batons drawn on
      Leicester crowd.
Aug: disorder in Burnley.
Sep: extraordinary events in Birkenhead: raids by police on
      working-class homes after clash between unemployed and
      officers;   many reports of people badly beaten;   over
      100 taken to hospital with severe injuries;   violence
      between police and jobless elsewhere on Merseyside and
      in London.
Oct: police charge demonstration in Glasgow;   violence in
      Croydon;   riots in London;   cameras forbidden to film
      NUWM 4th Hunger March;   marchers and police clash in
      Stratford-upon-Avon;   in Belfast police baton-charge
      march;   second march is banned, but goes ahead;
      widespread fighting;   barricades erected;   police
      stoned;   great violence by police;   two people shot
      dead by police, several more wounded;   troops called
      in;   Tom Mann, Hon. Treasurer of NUWM, arrested;
      disturbances at North Shields and West Ham;   disorder
      in Lambeth;   `uproar´ in Leicester;   at Hyde Park, it
      is claimed that special constables attack hunger
      marchers after abuse;   violent scenes ensue;   mounted

police charge into crowd;   70 public and 7 police injured;   three days later, in Trafalgar Square, trouble between police and demonstrators.

Nov: when NUWM petition is taken to Westminster violence occurs;   3174 police clash with unemployed;   fierce fighting;   police seize petition;   police raid NUWM headquarters, without a warrant, and confiscate documents;   damages and costs are later awarded against the police;   Wal Hannington, leader of NUWM, is arrested for incitement;   he is sentenced to 3 months in prison;   Home Secretary Gilmour warns Cabinet that during the recent disturbances `the position had become extremely critical´.

Dec: Sid Elias, Chairman of NUWM, gets 2 years in prison for sedition;   Tom Mann and Emrys Llewellyn (NUWM secretary) each sentenced to 2 months in prison.

1933

Jan: unemployment reaches 3 million. .
Feb: 20,000 in TUC demonstration at Hyde Park.
Mar: disorder when Prince of Wales visits Glasgow.
Apr: means test riot in Durham.
May: violent clashes between fascists and opponents in London;   violent anti-Hitler demonstration in London;   more trouble at fascist rally in London;   unemployed storm meeting in London;   clash between police and jobless in Great Yarmouth.
Nov: violence between Blackshirts and others in Coventry;   trouble at fascist meeting in London.

1934

Feb: 5th National Hunger March underway;   National Council for Civil Liberties formed by, amongst others, Attlee, Brittain, Herbert, Laski, and Wells.
Mar: trouble with fascists in Bristol;   serious street disorder in Glasgow (1 dead, 3 injured).
Apr: fight in Newcastle between fascists and communists.
Jun: disturbance at BUF meeting at Olympia;   anti-fascist demonstrators beaten up;   many badly injured;   disturbance at BUF meeting in Finsbury Park;   police use batons in Plymouth at clash between BUF supporters and opponents;   disorder after Blackshirt meeting in Leicester;   trouble and arrests at BUF meeting in Sheffield.
Jul: Cabinet discusses proposals for strengthening public order law.
Sep: trouble at BUF meeting in Leicester.
Oct: disorder at fascist rally in Plymouth.
Nov: Incitement to Disaffection Act receives Royal Assent.

1935

Jan: agitation against the new unemployment relief scales.
Feb: protests all over the country; in South Wales, 300,000 on the streets; disturbances at Merthyr, Arbertillery, Nantyglo and Blaina; large scale protests in Yorkshire and Scotland; heavy fighting in Sheffield; trouble in Tyneside and Lancashire; MP attacked in Lincoln; new scales withdrawn.
Apr: crowd stone police in South Wales; trouble at BUF meeting in Leicester.
Jun: police baton charge in Belfast; woman dies at Blackshirt meeting in Bootle; Stanley Baldwin becomes Prime Minister.
Jul: Orange disorders in Glasgow; riots in Belfast.
Oct: violence at fascist meeting in Leicester.
Nov: stormy scenes at election meetings; in the general election Labour win 154 seats (gain of 102), Conservatives win 437.

1936

Mar: trouble at fascist meeting at Albert Hall; police accused of attacking anti-fascists.
May: disturbances at BUF meetings in Oxford and Leicester.
Jun: further disorder at BUF meeting in Oxford and in Manchester.
Jul: disturbances at BUF rally in Hull; trouble on Orange march in Glasgow.
Aug: disorder at BUF meetings in Bristol and Leicester.
Sep: violence at fascist rally in Leeds.
Oct: British Union of Fascists march in East End is confronted by crowd estimated at 100,000; fighting ensues; in the `Battle of Cable Street´ many are injured, over 80 arrested; Jarrow `Crusade´ arrives in London; unemployment in Jarrow is 73 per cent; march receives much favourable publicity; 6th National Hunger March by NUWM arrives in London; although much bigger than Jarrow `Crusade´, it receives less attention.
Dec: Public Order Act receives Royal Assent.

1937

Apr: City Road Police Station reports continued disturbances in the East End.
May: Neville Chamberlain becomes Prime Minister.
Jun: further attacks by fascists on Jews.
Jul: Irishmen riot in Huddersfield; very serious disturbances in Bermondsey and south London at BUF march; 113 arrests and 28 casualties.
Oct: fascist riot in Liverpool.
Nov: commotion at the Cenotaph.

1938

Mar: uproar at Leicester meeting.
May: Mosley's Leicester headquarters stormed.
Jun: reports of anti-semitic attacks and abuse in various areas.
Dec: 200 men sit down in Oxford Street, with banners saying `work or bread´, Ritz is occupied by unemployed asking for tea for twopence.

1939

Jan: unemployed threaten police in Brighton; invasions continue of expensive restaurants in Piccadilly and Regent Street; several `chain-gangs´ are arrested, after chaining themselves to public buildings.
May: further reports of attacks on Jews.
Jul: rent strikers fight with police in Middlesex; crowd tries to lynch Irishman in Liverpool disorder.
Aug: trouble at peace demonstration in Downing Street.
Sep: war against Germany is declared.
Nov: disorder at fascist meeting in London.

Sources:

Charles Mowat, **Britain between the Wars**, Methuen, 1968

Peter Kingsford, **The Hunger Marchers in Britain 1920-1940**, Lawrence and Wishart, 1982

John Stevenson and Chris Cook, **The Slump**, Quartet, 1979

Dr Ivan Waddington, Department of Sociology, University of Leicester